The Names Book
Using Names to Teach Reading, Writing, and Math in the Primary Grades

by

Dorothy P. Hall and Patricia M. Cunningham

Carson–Dellosa Publishing Company, Inc.

Greensboro, North Carolina

Editors: Erin Seltzer and Joey Bland

Layout Design: Jon Nawrocik

Inside Illustrations: Mike Duggins

Cover Design: Annette Hollister-Papp

Cover Illustration: Lisa Olsen

Printed in the USA / All rights reserved.   ISBN 1-59441-027-5

The Names Book

Table of Contents

Why Use Children's Names?

Names are a source of fascination for all of us. Parents spend hours pondering names for their soon-to-be-born babies. Members of the family hope for "namesakes." Everyone notices and comments on names.

"What an unusual name!"

"That name suits her exactly."

"He has a strong name and a personality to match."

"His name doesn't really suit him."

"A lovely name and a lovely girl!"

Young children are also fascinated with names. They play with their names and the names of their friends—often pairing them with rhymes:

"Silly Billy"

"Bad Brad"

"Fancy Nancy"

Or with adjectives with the same beginning sound:

"Jumping Jim"

"Pesky Pat"

"Dancing Dottie"

As children get older, they create nicknames for each other. Robert becomes "Skippy," "Slick," or "Shorty." In their teen years, as children take on new identities, they often adopt different forms of their names. Maggie becomes "Meg" and Geneva becomes "Genie."

Young children are always curious about names. Within seconds of meeting you, they will ask, "What's your name?" If you have a dog, they immediately ask about the dog's name. Given just a little encouragement, they will share with you the names of all their family members, pets, and dolls.

Teachers can capitalize upon this universal interest in names by using names to teach a whole variety of concepts. Print concepts include the difference between letters and words, the left-to-right sequencing of letters in words, and the importance of having all the letters in exactly the right order. Students learn these concepts easily when the words being used to teach them use children's names and other important-to-them names. Letter names and sounds are easy to remember when they are connected to names. Even math operations, counting, adding and subtracting, for example, engage the attention of children when their names and the names of their friends are the basis for the mathematical problems.

We began using children's names to teach these and other abstract concepts many years ago. Before using the names of the children to "anchor" the concept being taught, we noticed how quickly children "forgot" concepts they had recently seemed to master. Children who could name and provide sounds for many letters before the winter holiday often returned to school having forgotten everything they had learned. Once we began using their names, however, children retained the beginning reading and math concepts more easily. Children paid better attention to the activities when their names were used and they associated these new and arbitrary concepts with the people, pets, products, and places so important to their world.

In this book, we have collected a variety of activities teachers have used to teach important literacy and math concepts using names. We hope you will find they create interest and enthusiasm in your children as they have in children in our classrooms. We are sure that once you begin to use some of the activities with your children, you will think of other engaging name activities. We would love to hear how the names activities in this book and other names activities you discover succeed in motivating and engaging your children.

Dottie Hall
halldp@wfu.edu

Pat Cunningham
cunningh@wfu.edu

Teaching Print Concepts with Names

Chapter 1

One essential part of the foundation for learning to read is the ability to track print. Another essential part is the ability to notice the first word or the last letter or the fact that **Robert** and **Rasheed** begin with the same letter. These print concepts are essential to successfully beginning the journey toward literacy and, in turn, are some of the most important concepts to focus on during the first month of school. Many teachers assess and monitor children's development of print concepts with a checklist which includes:

• Starts on the left

• Goes left to right

• Makes return sweep to next line

• Matches words by pointing to each as reading

• Can point to just one word

• Can point to the first word and the last word

• Can point to just one letter

• Can point to the first letter and the last letter

Teachers use the checklist as children participate in shared reading and the Comparing Names and Getting to Know You activities in this chapter. As different children volunteer to read, the teacher asks them to point to what they are reading. She also asks them if they can show just one word, point to the first and last word, show just one letter, and point to the first and last letters of a word. If they are successful, she puts a plus in the column showing what they have demonstrated. When children have two pluses in a column from two different days, the teacher assumes this child has the concept and does not check this concept anymore for this child. When children demonstrate that they have all these concepts, the teacher draws a line through their names and focuses the instruction and assessment on children who have not yet demonstrated these concepts.

Teachers put minuses in the columns of students who are not yet successful, so that they know to continue to give them practice and watch their progress. Many teachers work individually or in a small group with children who still have not mastered these concepts by rereading big books, charts, and focusing on these concepts.

Print concepts can be developed using many common activities including morning message and shared reading. In this chapter, we describe two activities you can use to capitalize on children's interest in names to develop print concepts.

Comparing Names with a Names Board

In this activity, all the children's first names (with initials for last names if two names are the same) will be written with a permanent marker on sentence strips. Once the name is written, we cut the strips so that long names have long strips and short names, short strips. We do not write these names ahead of time because it is important for the children to watch while the names are being written. To begin the activity, gather the children close to the pocket chart and explain what is going to happen. Say, "This is your classroom and you are the most important people here. We are going to make a bulletin board with all of your names (and pictures) and use these names to begin learning about letters and words."

Choose a child and write that child's name on a sentence strip as everyone watches. If the child can, invite that child to help you spell the name. After writing each name, display it in a pocket chart or other board. As you put each name up, comment on letters shared by certain children or other common features:

"**David**'s name begins and ends with the same letter. The **d** looks different because one is a capital **D** and the other is a small **d** (or uppercase/lowercase—whatever jargon you use.)"

"**Rasheed**'s name starts with the same letter as **Robert**'s name."

"**Bo**'s name only takes two letters to write. He has the shortest name but he is one of the tallest boys."

"We have two **Ashleys** so I will have to put the first letter of her last name—**M.**— so that we will know which **Ashley** this is."

You want the children to watch and think as the names are being written. Students usually will watch closely because they are so interested in themselves and each other. Their attention for anything, however, diminishes after 15-20 minutes. If you have a large class, you may want to write the names during two different sessions. Once you have written all the names, ask volunteers to come and find a name they can read. Many children will read their own names and almost everyone will remember Bo!

Display these names on a bulletin board. Many teachers add photos to go with the names and this addition makes an especially captivating display.

To prepare for comparing names on a names board, write each child's name again on an index card or a piece of sentence strip. (The children do not need to watch you writing these the second time.) Put the names in a box or a hat so that you can draw names randomly and focus children's attention on them. Gather the children together. Show them the container with names and tell them that you are going to draw out a name and see who can figure out whose name it is. Reach into the container and pull out a name. Show it to the children and let everyone who can "shout out (or whisper) the name" do so. Have the child whose name was drawn take the name to the names board and match it to be sure it is the right name. Have this child point to the letters in his name and lead everyone to count and then say the letters.

Then, let the child lead the class in comparing his name to all the names on the names board. Prompt children to make responses using the jargon you are teaching. You want children to make responses such as:

"Kathleen has **more letters** than David."

"Kathleen and David both have an **a**."

"The a is the **second letter** in Kathleen and David."

"Kathleen and Kevin **begin with** the **same letter**."

"The **last letter** in Kathleen and Kevin are the **same** too."

Continue pulling names from the container, having everyone identify the name, count the letters and name the letters. Let each child take her name to the names board and call on children to tell what they notice about that child's name and other names. After 15-20 minutes, bring this activity to a halt, assuring children that you will pull more names tomorrow and continue until every child's name has been the object of everyone's undivided attention.

Getting to Know You Charts

Most teachers begin their year with some get-acquainted activities. As part of these get-acquainted activities, they often have a special child each day. If you interview each child and write a chart summarizing important facts about that child, you can use that chart to develop print tracking skills.

If you did the Comparing Names activity described in this chapter, you can use the second set of sentence strip names. If not, prepare for this activity by writing all the children's first names (with initials for last names if two names are the same) with a permanent marker on sentence strips. Cut the strips so that long names have long strips and short name have short strips. Let the children watch you write their names and have them help you spell their names if they can. After writing each name, place all the names in a hat, box, or bag.

Tell children that each day, one of them will be the special child. Explain that in order to make it fair—since some children will have to wait 20 days or more—you are going to shake up the names in the box and, without looking, draw one of the names. Tell the children what the special child will get to do each day. Some teachers crown that child king or queen, let them lead the line, decide what game to play for P. E., sit in a special chair to greet visitors, pass things out, or have other special roles. Do keep in mind that whatever you do for the first student you must do for all the rest, so make sure you can sustain whatever you start. (Remember the, "Don't do anything the first month of marriage you don't want to do the whole rest of your married life," advice most of us got but ignored!) Each day, reach into the box and draw out a name. This child becomes the special child and the focus of many literacy activities. For our example, we will assume that Kathleen is the first name pulled from the box.

When Kathleen's name comes out, have her come forward and sit in a special chair. Appoint the rest of the class members to be reporters. Their job is to interview Kathleen and find out what she likes to eat, play, and do after school. Does she have brothers? Sisters? Cats? Dogs? Mice? Decide on a certain number of questions (5-7) and call on different children to ask questions.

Kathleen likes to read.

Kathleen likes to go bowling.

She likes to watch baseball.

She likes to eat chocolate cake.

Kathleen has a brother named Ryan.

She has a big cat named Squeaky.

After the interview, write your "newspaper article" on this special child using a shared writing format in which the children give suggestions and you and they decide what to say first, last, etc. Record this article on a chart while the children watch. Since these articles will be some of the first material most children will be able to read, make sure the articles have simple sentences and no more than 5-6 lines. The interview and the writing should be completed in the 20 minute attention span. If the teacher limits the number of questions and leads in the writing of the article, this timing is possible.

Once the chart is written, lead the class in a shared reading of the chart. Let Kathleen point to each word as everyone reads the article. Help her track print if she needs guidance. Once students have read the chart, ask questions that lead them to develop print concepts and print tracking skills. Here are some possible questions:

"Who can come and show us all the words in the first sentence?"

"Who can come and show us all the words in the last sentence?"

"Who can come and show us the longest sentence?"

"The shortest sentence?"

"Who can come and count the number of times we see Kathleen's name?"

"Can you find some other words in the chart that are used more than once?"

Lead the children to read Kathleen's chart chorally several times and let volunteers come and read each sentence. Guide their hands so that they track print as they read.

Most teachers display each chart for five days and then let the child take the chart home, with instructions to display it on the child's bedroom door. This procedure ensures that there are only five charts in the room at any one time but every chart gets read and reread on five different days.

Many teachers also write or type the sentences from the chart. After all the children have had their special days and been interviewed, the teacher compiles a class book containing each article along with a picture of each child. Each child then has one night to take the book home so that her family can get to know the whole class.

Another activity many teachers do with each name is giving the children an opportunity to focus on each name by writing it. We give each child a sheet of drawing paper and have them write the name of the special child in large letters on one side of the paper. We model at the board how to write each letter as they write the name but we do not expect their writing to look just like ours. We resist the temptation to correct what they wrote. Early in the year, children who have not written much will reverse letters and make them in funny ways. The important understanding is that names are words, that words can be written, and that it takes lots of letters to write them. We are giving them a kinesthetic way to focus on the word. While we model correct handwriting, we do not, at this point, expect correct letter formation from everyone.

After they write the name in whatever fashion they can, children turn the paper over and draw a picture of that child on the other side of the drawing paper. Let the special child of the day take all the pictures home!

As students become familiar with each name, some teachers suggest that they can write the name or, if they choose to, write one of the chart sentences or one of their own sentences about the child of the day before drawing. Children who come to first grade with more writing ability often enjoy copying one of the chart sentences or making up one of their own and other children enjoy trying to write the name and drawing the picture.

Learning to read is a complex task. There are arbitrary rules about starting on the left and moving right. When you finish a line, you have to return to the left and start again to read the next line. Spaces indicate the end of one word and the beginning of the next word. Children need to learn these and other print tracking skills. Charts that focus on children and their names are high-interest materials to teach these skills.

In addition to tracking print, children must learn the meaning of a lot of print-related jargon. Terms like word, sentence, and letter are often confusing to beginning readers. Things get even more complicated when teachers ask them to look at the first letter or the last letter or the first word or the last word or the first sentence or the last sentence. Because children find names so interesting, teachers can use names to build their understanding of this critical print jargon. Making a class names board, comparing the names, and writing getting to know you charts use names to do just that—develop children's awareness of print concepts.

Teaching Phonemic Awareness with Names

Chapter 2

Children who have phonemic awareness can manipulate words. They can clap syllables in words and know that the word **motorcycles** takes more claps than the word **car**. Students with phonemic awareness can stretch out words and tell you what word you stretched out. They can tell you that **bike** rhymes with **Mike** and that **book** doesn't. After enjoying and participating in *There's a Wocket in My Pocket!* (Dr. Seuss, Random House Books for Young Readers, 1974) activities, they can make up silly rhymes for objects in the classroom. They can get *The Hungry Thing* (Jan Slepian and Ann Seidler, Scholastic, Inc., 2001) to eat their food by making up a word that rhymes with what they want to feed it.

We assess children's phonemic awareness by observing their ability to do these rhyming word tasks as we do the activities with the whole class. Just as for print concepts, we would require two pluses on two different days before deciding they had developed the concept. Phonemic awareness is not a single concept and is not an easy concept for many children. Not all children will have all parts of it, even after several months. As we moved into more advanced decoding and spelling activities, we would know which ones needed continued nudges toward developing this awareness.

These three practical books give you lots of fun activities for helping children develop phonemic awareness:

Phonemic Awareness: Playing with Sounds to Strengthen Beginning Reading Skills by Jo Fitzpatrick, et al. (Creative Teaching Press, 1997)

Phonics through Poetry: Teaching Phonemic Awareness Using Poetry by Babs Bell Hajdusiewicz (Goodyear Publishing Company, 1998)

The Phonological Awareness Handbook for Kindergarten and Primary Teachers by Lila Ericson and Moira Juliebo (International Reading Association, 1998)

Hearing Rhyming Words

Choose the children whose names have lots of rhyming words to come forward. Say a word that rhymes with one of the names and have the children say the word along with the name of the rhyming child.

When you have a one-syllable name with which there are many rhymes (Pat, Tran, Joe, Sue, etc.), seize the opportunity to help the children listen for words that rhyme with that name. Say pairs of words, some of which rhyme with **Mike**, for example.

Mike/ball   Mike/bike   Mike/hike   Mike/cook   Mike/like

If the pairs rhyme, everyone should point to Mike and whisper, "MIKE." If not, they should shake their heads and frown.

Blending and Segmenting Words

In addition to hearing and producing rhyme, the ability to put sounds together to make a word—blending—and the ability to separate the sounds in a word—segmenting—are critical components of phonemic awareness. Blending and segmenting are not easy for many children. In general, it is easier for them to segment the beginning sound, the onset, from the rest of the word, the rime, than it is to separate all the sounds. In other words, children can usually separate **bat** into **b-at** before they can produce the three sounds **b-a-t**. The same is true for blending. Most children can blend **S-am** to produce the name **Sam** before they can blend **S-a-m**. Most teachers begin by having children blend and segment the onset from the rime. Then, the teachers have children blend and segment individual letters.

An activity to help children segment words into onsets is matching beginning sounds in names. Say a sound, not a letter, and have all the children whose names begin with that sound come forward. Stretch out the sound as you make it "s-s-s-s" For the "s-s-s" sound, **Samantha**, **Susie**, **Steve**, and **Cynthia** should all come forward. Have everyone stretch out the "s-s-s" as they say the names. If anyone points out that **Cynthia** starts with a **C** or that **Sharon** starts with an **S**, explain that they are correct about the letters but that now you are listening for sounds.

There are lots of games children enjoy that can help them learn to blend and segment. The most versatile one is a simple riddle guessing game. The teacher begins the game by naming the category and giving a clue:

"I'm thinking of an animal that lives in the water and is a **f-ish** (or **f-i-sh** depending on what level of blending you are working on)."

The child who correctly guesses "fish" gives the next riddle:

"I'm thinking of an animal that goes quack and is a **d-uck** (or **d-u-ck**)."

This game sounds simple but children love it. You can use different categories to go along with units you are studying. A wonderful variation on this guessing game is to put objects in a bag and let children reach in the bag and stretch out the name of the object they chose. Then, they call on someone to guess "What is it?" Choose small common objects you find in the room, a cap, a ball, chalk, or a book, for example, and let the children help you stretch out the words for practice as you fill the bag.

Children also like to talk like "ghosts." One child chooses an object in the room to say as a ghost would—stretching the word out very slowly without repeating the individual sounds— "**d-or**." The child who correctly guesses **door** gets to ghost talk another object without repeating the individual sounds—"**b-oo-k**." Both the ghost talk game and the guessing game provide practice in both segmenting and blending as children segment words by stretching them out and other children blend the words together to guess them.

Sound Boxes

Some children find segmenting words into sounds very difficult. Many students have found success using a technique called sound boxes in which children push chips, pennies or other object into boxes as they hear the sounds. In the first lessons, children have a drawing of three boxes.

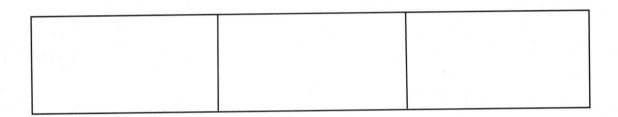

The teacher says familiar words composed of three sounds such as **cat**, **sun**, **dog**, **pan**. Often children are shown pictures of these objects. After naming each object, the teacher and children "stretch out" the three sounds, distorting the word as little as possible—"**s-u-n.**" Children push a chip into each box as they say that part of the word. It is important to note here that the boxes represent sounds (phonemes)—not letters. Children's names are ideal for sound boxes. You can use 3 sound boxes for **Pat**, **Sam**, **Deb**, **Tom**, etc. You can also use names like **Joey**, **Pete**, and **Jack**. These names have three sounds, but four letters, so they would be segmented into three sound boxes as well. Once children get good at segmenting words with three sounds, they are given a drawing with four boxes and they stretch out some four-phoneme names such as **Molly**, **Erin**, **Chad**, and **Marie**.

Sound boxes are used extensively to develop phonemic awareness in children in Reading Recovery™ (Clay, 1985). Reading Recovery™ is a highly successful one-on-one tutoring program that works with first graders in the bottom 20% of the class. Once children can push the chips to represent sounds, Reading Recovery™ has them push letter cards into boxes. From the letters **m**, **p**, **s**, **t**, and **a**, the teacher could ask the children to push these letters to spell words such as **sat**, **Pat**, **tam**, **Sam**, **Pam**, **mats**, and **maps**. Children only work with letters in the sound boxes after they have developed some phonemic awareness and are working on learning letter names and letter sounds. Later on children actually write the letters in the boxes as they attempt to spell words they are writing.

You can also segment names into sounds without each child having a drawing of sound boxes. Call children to line up by stretching out their names, emphasizing each of the sounds the letters make. As each child lines up, have the class stretch out the name with you.

Tongue Twisters and Books with Alliteration

In addition to the concepts of rhyme, blending and segmenting, children must learn what it means that words "start the same." This understanding must be in place before children can make sense of the notion that particular letters make particular sounds. Since, many children confuse the concept of words beginning with the same sound with the concept of rhyme, many teachers like to wait until the concept of rhyme is firmly established for most children before focusing on whether or not words "start the same". Just as for rhyme, we would build a lot of our work with words that start the same by choosing wonderful books such as *All about Arthur (An Absolutely Absurd Ape)* by Eric Carle (Franklin Watts, Inc., 1974). Arthur, an ape who plays the accordion, travels around the country meeting lots of other musicians including a bear who plays a banjo in Baltimore and a yak in Yonkers! In the classic *Dr. Seuss's ABC* (Dr. Seuss, Random House Books for Young Readers, 1963), each letter of the alphabet has a sentence such as "Many mumbling mice are making midnight music in the moonlight." This is another excellent example of an appealing book that helps children understand what it means to "start the same." When using books with alliteration, we would follow the same steps followed with rhyming books:

1. Read and enjoy the book several times.

2. Point out that the author used some "start the same" words to make the book fun to say and identify these words.

3. Let the children say the "start the same" words with us as we read the book again.

4. Have the children come up with other words that "start the same" that the author could have used on that page.

Once you have read and enjoyed several tongue twister books, create a tongue twister book for your class. Let children help you make up tongue twisters and add two or three more each day. Turn them into posters or bind them into a class book. Let the children read them with you several times as slow as they can and as fast as they can. Help children understand that what makes tongue twisters hard to say fast is that since the words all start the same, you keep having to get your mouth and tongue into the same place. The same first sound repeated over and over is also what makes them so much fun to say. Here are some tongue twisters to get you started. You and your children can surely make up better ones. Be sure to use children's names from your class when they have the right letters and sounds!

Billy's baby brother bopped Betty.

Carol can catch caterpillars.

David dozed during dinner.

Fred's father fell fifty feet.

Gorgeous Gloria gets good grades.

Hungry Harry hates hamburgers.

Jack juggled Jill's jewelry.

Kevin's kangaroo kicked Karen.

Louie likes licking lemon lollipops.

Mike's mom makes marvelous meatballs.

Naughty Nellie never napped nicely.

Patty prefers pink pencils.

Roger Rabbit runs relays.

Susie's sister sipped seven sodas.

Tom took ten turtles to town.

Veronica visited very vicious volcanoes.

Wild Willis went west.

Yippy yanked Yolanda's yellow yo-yo.

Zany Zeb zapped Zeke's zebra.

As you work with tongue twisters and books with lots of words that begin with the same letter, begin by emphasizing the words that start the same. This understanding is the phonemic awareness concept that underlies phonics knowledge. When your children can tell you whether or not words start with the same sound and can come up with other words that start that way, shift your instruction to which letter makes which sound. You can use the very same books and tongue twisters again, but this time emphasize the sound of the letter. Books with alliteration and tongue twisters help your children develop the important "starts the same" component of phonemic awareness and can help them learn some letter sounds.

Here are some wonderful tongue twister books:

ABCD: An Alphabet Book of Cats and Dogs by Sheila Moxley (Little, Brown & Company, 2001)

All about Arthur (An Absolutely Absurd Ape) by Eric Carle (Franklin Watts, Incorporated, 1974)

Alphabet Annie Announces an All-American Album by Marcia O'Shell & Susan Purviance (Houghton Mifflin Company, 1988)

Animalia by Graeme Base (Harry N. Abrams, 1987)

The Biggest Tongue Twister Book in the World by Gyles Brandeth (Sterling, 1983)

Dr. Seuss's ABC by Dr. Seuss (Random House Books for Young Readers, 1963)

Faint Frogs Feeling Feverish and Other Terrifically Tantalizing Tongue Twisters by Lilian Obligada (Viking Children's Books 1986)

Four Famished Foxes and Fosdyke by Pamela Duncan Edwards (HarperTrophy, 1997)

Six Sick Sheep: One Hundred One Tongue Twisters by Joanna Cole (Beech Tree Books, 1993)

Some Smug Slug by Pamela Duncan Edwards (HarperTrophy, 1998)

A Twister of Twists, A Tangler of Tongues: Tongue Twisters by Alvin Schwartz (Harpercollins Juvenile Books, 1991)

Counting Words

To count words, all children should have ten counters in a paper cup. (Anything children can manipulate is fine. Some teachers use edibles such as raisins, grapes, or small crackers and let the children eat their counters at the end of the lesson. This makes clean-up quick and easy!) Begin by counting some familiar objects in the room (windows, doors, trash cans, etc.) and have all children place one of their counters on their desks as each object is pointed to. Have children return counters to the cup before beginning to count each object.

Tell children that you can also count words by putting down a counter for each word you hear. Explain that you will say a sentence in the normal way and then repeat the sentence, pausing after each word. The children should put down counters as you slowly say the words in the sentence, and then count the counters to decide how many words you said. As usual, children's attention is better if you make sentences about them. (Carol has a big smile. Paul is back at school today. I saw Jack at church.) Once the children catch on to the activity, let them say some sentences, first in the normal way, then one word at a time. Listen carefully as they say their sentences the first time because they will often need help saying them one word at a time. Children enjoy this activity, and not only are they learning to separate words in speech, they are also practicing critical counting skills!

Clapping Syllables

Once children can automatically separate the speech stream into words, they are ready to begin thinking about separating words into some components. The first division most children learn to make is that of syllables. Clapping seems the easiest way to get every child involved, and children's names are naturally appealing words to clap. Say the first name of one child. Say the name again, and this time, clap the syllables. Continue saying first names and clapping the syllables. As you say names the second time, invite the children to clap with you. Once children begin to understand, clap the beats and have all the children whose names have that number of beats stand and say their names as they clap the beats with you. As children catch on, say some middle or last names. The term **syllables** is a little jargony and foreign to most young children, so you may want to refer to the syllables as beats. Children should realize by clapping that **Paul** is a one-beat word, **Miguel** is a two-beat word, and **Madeira** is a three-beat word.

Once children can clap syllables and decide how many beats a given word has, help them to see that one beat words are usually shorter than three beat words—that is, they take fewer letters to write. To do this, write on sentence strips some words children cannot read and cut the strips so that short words have short strips and long words have long strips. Have some of the words begin with the same letters but be different lengths so that children will need to think about word length to decide which word is which.

For the category animals, you might write **horse** and **hippopotamus**, **dog** and **donkey**, **kid** and **kangaroo**; **rat**, **rabbit**, and **rhinoceros**. Tell the children that you are going to say the names of animals and they should clap to show how many beats the word has. (Do not show them the words yet!) Say the first pair, one at a time (**horse/hippopotamus**). Help children to decide that **horse** is a one-beat word and **hippopotamus** takes a lot more claps and is a five-beat word. Now, show them the two words and say, "One of these words is **horse** and the other is **hippopotamus**. Who thinks they can figure out which one is **horse** and which one is **hippopotamus**?" Help the children by explaining that because **hippopotamus** takes so many beats to say it, it probably takes more letters to write it. Continue with other pairs of words—and finally with a trio to challenge your stars!

Phonemic awareness is not just another word for phonics. Phonemic awareness is the ability to take words apart, put them back together again, and change them. Phonemic awareness activities are done orally, calling attention to the sounds, not the letters or which letter makes which sound. Phonemic awareness activities help children hear and produce rhyme, put sounds together to make words, separate words to isolate sounds, hear words that "start the same," and orally isolate words and syllables. When children have developed phonemic awareness, they are ready to learn individual letters and their sounds.

Teaching Letter Names with Names

Chapter 3

Learning the names of all the letters seems like a simple enough task for adults but this task is a very difficult task for many children. One reason learning letter names is difficult is that the names are totally arbitrary. Why should the letter **a** be called "a?" Why do people call a letter a "d" when the circle is on the left, but when it is on the right, people call that letter a "b?" Another cause for confusion is that so many of the letter names sound just like words children know. Children know what a **bee** is—it can sting you. They know that **tea** is what you drink and **see** is what you do with your eyes. **I**, **you**, and **are** are words they use every day. Perhaps they know the names **Dee**, **Jay**, and **Kay**. These common sound-alike words add to the confusion many children experience when trying to remember which letter is called what.

Cheering the Names

One activity we have found highly successful in helping children learn letter names is to have them chant the spelling of each other's names. We call this cheering for the child and everyone loves to do it. Just get into your high-school-sports-events mode and you will know exactly how to choreograph this activity. Pompoms are optional but lots of fun! There are lots of ways you might do this cheering, but it is very important that the children are paying attention to the letters as they say them. Many teachers use large index cards to make letter posters—lowercase on one side and uppercase on the other. Unless you have a child with three of the same letters in her name, two cards for each letter is usually enough to cheer for all the children in the class. Display all the letter cards in alphabetical order along the chalk ledge or lay the cards on the floor. Put the duplicate of each letter behind the card and choose a child. Let that child find his or her name somewhere in the room, point to each letter, and choose someone to hold each letter card in his or her name.

The children chosen arrange themselves in the correct order. Each child holds up his letter and leads the cheer for that letter:

"Give me a J." (Everyone yells, "J!")

"Give me an a." (Everyone yells, "A!")

"Give me an s." (Everyone yells, "S!")

"Give me an m." (Everyone yells, "M!")

"Give me an i." (Everyone yells, "I!")

"Give me an n." (Everyone yells, "N!")

"Give me an e." (Everyone yells, "E!")

"What does it spell?" (Everyone one yells, "Jasmine!")

We call this the cheerleading game and young children love it. Be sure to give everyone a chance to be cheered for—including yourself. When the children cheer for you, choose some of the children not often picked to be the cheerleaders so that everyone has a chance to hold up letters and lead the cheer.

Over the course of cheering all the names, most of the letters will be used and reused thus giving the children lots of practice with the letters. If there are a few letters that don't occur in any names, designate a stuffed animal the class mascot. Make up a name for the mascot that includes the missing letters. One class of children loved cheering for their stuffed kangaroo mascot named Quevizy!

Sorting and Graphing Names

One of the activities suggested in the math chapter (Chapter 12, page 122) is counting and graphing the letters in each name. This activity also helps children focus on the names of letters. Make a graph from A to Z. Give each child his or her name card or have them wear their name necklaces. Start with the letter **a** and have everyone who has the letter **a** anywhere in his name come forward to be counted. Count all of the **a**'s including both **a**'s in **Alexander**. Let the children with **a**'s in their names color one square per letter **a** on the graph. Continue with the **b**'s, **c**'s etc. Children come forward every time their names include that letter. **Alexander** gets to come forward and add to the graph many times. Poor **Bo** may be feeling a little sorry since he has such a short name. Perhaps **Bo** could be assigned the job of bringing **Quevizy** up each time the letters in her name need to be counted.

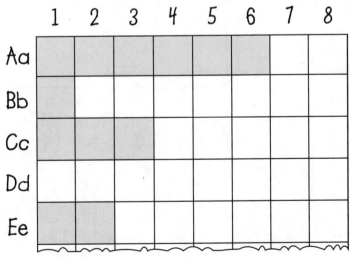

When the graph is completed, help the children think about which letters occur most and least in everyone's names. A nice homework assignment is to give everyone an A-Z graph to take home. (A reproducible A-Z graph is on page 136.) Have each child write his name and then graph his own letters. When students take their graphs home, they should write the names of family members and pets and graph the letters for them.

When the children bring their graphs back, compare them to the class graph. Do most of the graphs have lots of t's, s's, e's and i's and not many q's and z's. Could this explain why Wheel of Fortune® contestants always guess these common letters first?

Wheel of Names

Speaking of Wheel of Fortune®, children love playing a similar game we call Wheel of Names to guess names. Simply draw lines for the correct number of letters for one of the names in your class. Let children take turns asking for letters and filling them in. If she gets a "yes," a child keeps guessing. If she gets a "no," the next child guesses.

"Is there a t?"

("No," turn passes to next child.)

"Is there an e?"

("No," turn passes to next child.)

"Is there an n?"

("Yes," same child guesses again.)

"Is there an o?"

("Yes," same child guesses again.)

"Is there an a?"

("No," turn passes to next child.)

"Is there an h?"

("Yes," same child guesses again.)

"Is there a J?" "Yes!"

Wheel of Names is a lot of fun to play and you have to use your letter name knowledge to play.

Learning letter names can be difficult for many children. Cheering names, graphing names, and playing Wheel of Names are motivating ways to help children learn the names of letters.

Teaching Phonics with Names

Chapter 4

Your brain has a marvelous ability to remember things—thousands and thousands of things! Did you ever wonder how peoples' brains can store so many facts, experiences and ideas? When psychologists talk about how brains work, they often call the brain the "associative memory store." All the things people store in their memories are associated with other things. If your best friend was from Quebec, lots of your Quebec/Canada information relates to information about and memories of your friend. Seeing plum tomatoes in the produce section may bring back all your wonderful memories of Italy and the delicious food you enjoyed there. People can capitalize on their brains' abilities to quickly retrieve information when that information is already associated with something important. Using names to teach basic letter/sound correspondences does just that. A child who thinks of David whenever he sees the letter **d** can quickly retrieve the common sound for the letter **d**. The letter **p** might call up memories of Pizza Hut® and along with memories of yummy food, a child can easily retrieve the sound commonly associated with **p**. A Sesame Street® fan can retrieve common sounds for the vowel **e** by thinking of Elmo® and Ernie®, for example.

Names as Key Words on Names Boards

Many publishing companies and reading series include some key words for the common letter sounds but often children call the word something other than what is intended. Children call a dog "puppy" or a rabbit "bunny," for example, and the key words confuse rather than support their learning of letter sounds. You can use the names of the children in your class as key words for many of the common sounds. Make a grid on a bulletin board and put all the letters from A-Z in each square in alphabetical order. Add your children's names and pictures to your board a few at a time. Begin with the names of your children that have the most common sound associated with that letter. The first names added should have beginning letters with very different sounds. If possible save the names with blends (**st**, **br**, etc.) until later. If you happen to have **Jim**, **Joey**, **Pat**, **Michelle**, **Marie**, and **Karen** in your classroom, **J**, **P**, **M**, and

K would be good letters to begin with. Save the confusing letters for later. If **Carol** and **Carl** are the only two children you have whose name begins with **c**, you can add this letter early, but if you also have **Charlie** and **Cynthia**, leave the letter **c** until all of the easier letters for your class's names have been added. If you have a **Juan** or a **José**, you will want to wait to add the **j** until later.

Capitalize on children's interest in names by asking them to imagine that a new student is coming to join the class. Challenge them to figure out what letter that child's name begins with. Let's say that your names board looks like this to begin with:

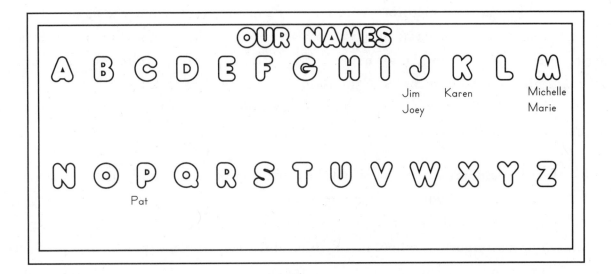

Say other names that begin like those names already on the board. Let your class decide which letter the new name begins with. As you say each new name, have children compare it with the names already on the board.

Here is a list of new names you might use if **J**, **K**, **M**, and **P** have key names on your board:

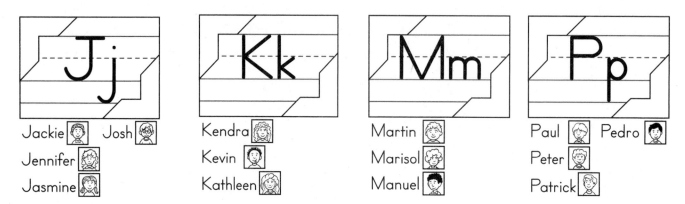

Continue to add names and pictures—your children's names, your name, the name of your assistant (if you have one), the name of the class mascot or pet, the principal's name, the names of special teachers—all the important names in your classroom community. As you add names, play the "imagine a new child comes to the room" game and have children decide what the first letter in that child's name would be. Add names with single consonants first and then add names like **Greg** and **Stephanie** that begin with blends.

Of course, each classroom's names board will be different and this year's board will be very different from next year's. Let your children's names and the grade level you teach jointly guide you about which letters and letter combinations to teach. By using the names and pictures of your children, other important school members, and names of people, places, and products your children recognize, you give your children tangible links to the common letter-sound relationships. You build the board gradually and add to it as the year goes on. Most teachers keep the board up all year and refer to it when children need to remember particular letter-sound relationships as they are reading and writing. The brain's memory system is based on association. Children who learn phonics by associating letters with important-to-them names are able to easily retrieve the common sounds for these letters when they need them.

The names you use should be determined by the children in your classroom and the number of phonics relationships you want to teach. Add names and pictures gradually, beginning with the names and pictures of people in your school community. Since no child should be left off the board, be sure to include all the names of your children—even if that means having three J names and names which do not represent the common sounds for all the letters. When you have all your important local names on the board, you can add other recognizable names with pictures to provide key words for letters your names lack. Unlike when adding the children's names, when adding "famous" names, we pick only one to represent each sound not represented by the names of your children. Here is a possible list of some "recognizable names." We hope that you will use this list as a starting point but will choose the most recognizable name for YOUR children. The key word board will work best for you if you use the names of your children and then include a locally famous person, place, or product to represent a missing sound.

A	Ace Hardware®, Alexander (famous for his "terrible, horrible, very bad day"), Alpo®, Apple Jacks®, Arby's®
B	Barney®, Bert® and Big Bird® (Sesame Street®), Bob the Builder®, Bugs Bunny®
C	Cleo® (Between the Lions®), Cookie Monster® and the Count (Sesame Street®), Clifford®
C (s sound)	Cinderella®
Ch	Cheerios®, Chips Ahoy®
D	Daffy Duck®, Daisy Duck, Donald Duck®, Dennis the Menace® Domino's®
E	Easter bunny, Elmo® and Ernie®(Sesame Street®), Eckerd®
F	Franklin®, Fred Flintstone, Frog (Toad's buddy)
G	Garfield®, Gatorade®, Goldilocks, Goldfish®
G (j sound)	gingerbread man, Gold's Gym® (both sounds)
H	Hardee's®, Huckleberry Hound®
I	ice-cream sandwiches
J	Jell-o®
K	KitKat®, K-mart®, Kool-Aid®
L	Lifesavers®, Lionel® and Leona® (Between the Lions®)
M	McDonald's®, Mickey Mouse®, Minnie Mouse®
N	Nerds®
O	Oprah, Oreo®, Oscar® (Sesame Street®), Outback Steakhouse®

P	Peter Pan®, Peter Rabbit, Pizza Hut®, Porky Pig®, PowerPuff Girls®
Q	Quaker® Oatmeal
R	Roadrunner®, Rudolph® (reindeer)
S	Santa, Subway®, Superman®, Sylvester®
Sh	Shoney's®
T	Target®, Telly (Sesame Street®), Toad (Frog's friend), Tootsie Roll®
Th	Theo (Between the Lions®)
U	UPS®
V	vanilla wafers; Velveeta®
W	Wal-Mart®, Wendy's®, Mrs. Wishy Washy, Woody Woodpecker®
X	X-Men®
Y	Yogi Bear®, Yoo-hoo®
Z	Zoe (Sesame Street®)

Names Boards in Kindergarten

If you teach kindergarten and you have a **Charley**, you need to add his name to your names board along with the **ch,** but if you don't have anyone in your kindergarten class whose name begins with **ch**, it is probably better not to complicate things with that letter combination. Here is the board as it might look in a kindergarten classroom when all the children's and other important names that begin with consonant or consonant combinations have been added. Examples for **ch** and **th** are included because all of the children's names need to be on the board and this kindergarten contains a **Charlie** and a **Theodore**. **Sh** is not included because no child's name begins with this letter combination and kindergarten children are not generally expected to learn the **sh** combination.

The vowels in English are exceptionally complicated and can have many different sounds. For that reason, most kindergarten teachers save the names that begin with vowels until last and then put those names in the boxes for the vowels. When you add your children's names that begin with vowels, play the "imagine a new student moves in" game and have your imaginary new students' names use the same vowel sounds as those represented by the children in your classroom. Here is the board with all the names of the important people in one kindergarten class added. The children whose names begin with vowels are **Elizabeth**, **Arthur**, **Andrew,** and **Ivan**. You could pretend that new children coming to your classroom were named **Anthony**, **Arturo**, **Ethan**, **Ida**, and **Alexander**.

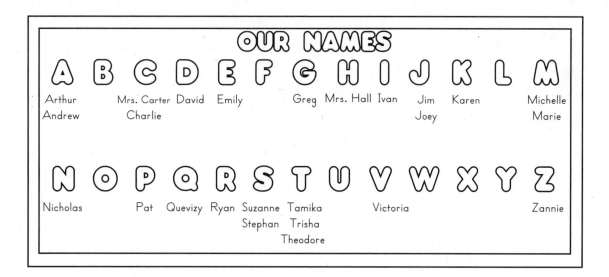

Once the board is complete with all the important names and pictures of your class, you may want to add some other familiar names of people, places, or products as key words for the letters your class doesn't have. We pick people or places all the children know and put their names and pictures in the appropriate boxes. Here is the completed board with key names and pictures for all of the letters except **x**. Unless you can think of a name your children would all recognize that begins with **x**, just tell your children there aren't any!

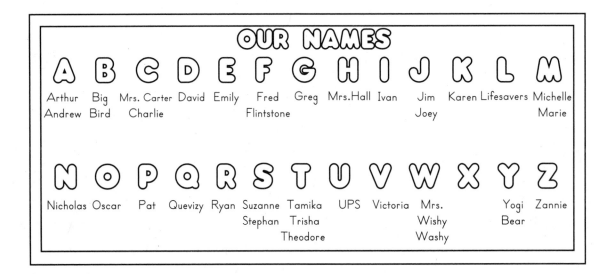

Names Boards in First and Second Grade

In first and second grade the same principles apply to beginning the names board. We add pictures with each name and we begin with the names of children in our classroom whose beginning letters are quite different from one another. We begin by adding names of children with single letters and then move to more complex letter combinations. In addition to children's names, we include the names and pictures of other important people and animals in our classroom community.

Here is what a first- or second-grade names board might look like when all the important names have been added.

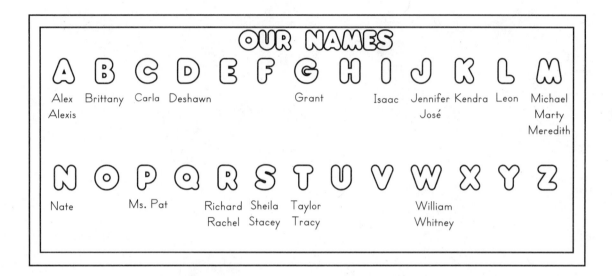

Since in first and second grades, we do want to teach all of the common letter combinations, we would add the names and pictures of some people, places or products to serve as key words for any sounds not represented by names in our immediate school community. Here is what the board might look like with these added names and pictures:

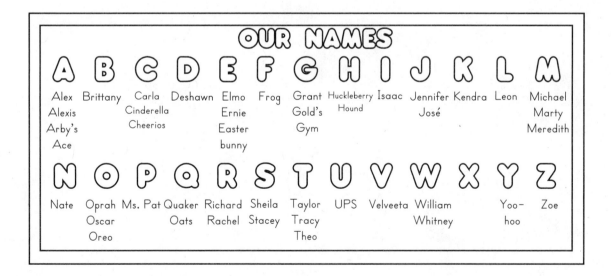

Using names as key words helps children easily retrieve common sounds for letters. Children's names, the names of familiar people, places, and products provide meaningful associations for letter/sound correspondence. Name boards are visual reminders of these important associations.

Alphabet Books with Names

Chapter 5

Alphabet books were some of the first books published for children. Most of the early alphabet books were simply written with just one word for each letter of the alphabet. Simple alphabet books with a word or words (they know) or a sentence or two on each page are still the best to read and use with young children. Alphabet books are once again popular and many have names in their titles.

There are lots of wonderful alphabet books to read and enjoy. Many of these fit into your themes or units of study. Research shows that the simple books with not too many words on a page and pictures that most of the children recognize are the most helpful to children in building letter-sound and letter-name knowledge. Once the book has been read and reread several times, children will enjoy reading it during their self-selected reading time. It is very important that children have time to choose and read books each day. Simple alphabet books, which have been read together, provide books that children can read on their own before they can read books with more text. We recommend the following books.

Recommended Alphabet Books

A, My Name is Alice by Jane Bayer (Puffin, 1992)

The alphabet text for this book comes from the playground games in grammar schools in the 1950s. ("A, my name is Alice, my husband's name is Alex, we come from Alaska and we sell ants.") The object was to think of and say a girl's name, boy's name, the name of a place to be from, and things to sell for each letter of the alphabet. Children did this as they bounced a ball. One leg went over the ball as you said the names. Read the alphabet book and your students will want to join in and make up their own ditties! ("**D**, my name is **D**ottie, my husband's name is **D**avid, we come from **D**enver, and we sell **d**ogs." See page 66 in Chapter 6, Interactive Charts with Names, for another idea for this book.)

Annie, Bea, and Chi Chi Delores: A School Day Alphabet by Donna Maurer (Orchard Books, 1998)
A school day trip through the alphabet from all aboard the school bus, to lining up and making music, and ending with a zip (of the jacket).

Aster Aardvark's Alphabet Adventures by Steven Kellogg (Mulberry Books, 1992)
Every page of the alphabet book is about an animal character whose first and last name begins with the same letter of the alphabet and is filled with words beginning with that same letter. ("Desperate for dinner after a day of digging up dinosaurs in the desert, Dr. Delphius Dog and a dozen dedicated disciples dined on delicious . . . .")

Black and White Rabbit's ABC by Alan Baker (Larousse Kingfisher Chambers, 1999)
Black and White Rabbit paints his way through the alphabet. Young children enjoy following Rabbit as he makes new discoveries with paint, a paintbrush, and the alphabet.

Curious George Learns the Alphabet by H. A. Rey (Houghton Mifflin Co., 1973)
Curious George, the little brown monkey who is always curious, learns the alphabet from his friend "the man with the yellow hat." Watch as he draws the letters of the alphabet and uses words that begin with this letter to tell a short story about each one.

Goodnight to Annie: An Alphabet Lullaby by Eve Merriam (Hyperion Press, 1999)
A nighttime alphabet book with animals and letters of the alphabet from A-Z for bedtime or school time reading. Each page has a large clear letter and sleep coming to all the creatures. (O Oysters are in their oyster beds.)

Harold's ABC by Crockett Johnson (HarperCollins Juvenile Books, 1981)
Harold and his purple crayon take another adventure, through the alphabet from A to Z, in this book.

Hooper Humperdink by Theodore LeSieg (Random House Books for Young Readers, 1976)
There's going to be a party and everyone will be invited but Hooper Humperdink. Who is asked? Alice and Abel; Bob, Bill and Babe; etc. This is an alphabet book of names written in rhyme, in typical Dr. Seuss style.

Miss Bindergarten Gets Ready for Kindergarten by Joseph Slate (Puffin, 2001)
This is an alphabet book written in rhyme about a kindergarten teacher getting ready for the
first day of kindergarten.

Miss Spider's ABC by David Kirk (Callaway Editions, 1998)
From ant to zebra an alphabet book of tongue twisters. Miss Spider's friends are preparing for
her surprise birthday party in this beautifully illustrated ABC book.

Paddington's ABC by Michael Bond (Puffin, 1996)
Paddington Bear shows young children that learning the alphabet can be fun as he holds an
apple, puts on his boots, takes a picture with a camera, feeds a duck, and eats an egg, etc. An
easy alphabet book for children to "picture read."

Peter Rabbit's ABC by Beatrix Potter (Viking Press, 1998)
Here are Peter Rabbit and all his friends in an alphabet book ("A is for apple. B is for butter. C
is for carrot.") that uses the original pictures.

What's Your Name? From Ariel to Zoe by Eve Sanders (Holiday House, 1995)
This is a book of names from all over the world. Some are long, some are short, some are old
favorites, and some of the names are new. In this book 26 children talk about themselves and
their names from A to Z.

Winnie-the-Pooh's ABC by A. A. Milne (Dutton Books, 1995)
Apple, balloon, cow, dragon . . . each letter of the alphabet is represented by an object from
Winnie the Pooh and the stories set in the Hundred Acre Woods.

Winnie the Pooh's A to Zzzz by Don Ferguson (Disney Press, 1992)
An alphabet book all about Winnie the Pooh and his friends; each letter represents something
that happens in the original book.

Making an ABC Book

Once you and the children have read several alphabet books, you might want to make an alphabet book centered around the names of children or things in your classroom. Have different children illustrate each page or take photos and put a simple caption on the bottom of each page. Some teachers just use one word on a page.

Instead of having just one word on a page, some teachers put the word and then a short sentence under it. Look around the room and see what you have for each letter. You may have to "plant" a few things you would not normally have in your classroom so they can be found when it is time to do that page. Classrooms are all different but here are some likely possibilities (with a few objects "planted" for obstinate letters like Q and X):

alphabet or arms

books, boys, or the board

computer, crayons, or a couch

desks, doors, or drawings

easel or ears

flag or feet

girls, gerbil, or glue

hands, hamster, or hammer

ivy or intercom

jackets, jump rope, or jars

keys or kangaroo (stuffed)

lunchboxes, Legos®, or legs

magazines or markers

numbers or noses

overhead or orange things

pencils, paint, paintbrushes, or paper

quilt or quarter

rug, rabbit, or red things

sink or scissors

teacher or television

umbrellas or Unifix® cubes

vase or violets

windows or walls

xylophone or the e<u>x</u>it sign

yardstick, yo-yo, or yellow things

zippers

You can make your school day alphabet book as a big book or you can make your school day alphabet book as an accordion alphabet book.

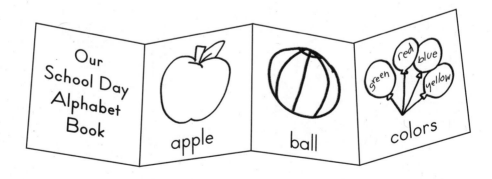

If you are studying insects, it may be an insect alphabet book. If you are studying animals, it may be an animal alphabet book.

Making Personal Dictionaries

Personal dictionaries are helpful to many students in first grade and after. Students label and illustrate pages with uppercase and lowercase letters. Then, they add the names of children in the class and words to each page as needed by writing the words and illustrating the words if needed.

For emergent readers, making alphabet books can help teach phonemic awareness and letters and sounds. In the book *Making Alphabet Books to Teach Letters and Sounds* (Dorothy Hall, Carson-Dellosa, 2001) each alphabet book page (using 26 letters and 35 sounds) begins with a tongue twister, uses the names of the children in your class (and other children's names when they are not represented!), predictable charts, and take-home alphabet books pages to teach children more about the alphabet. Making alphabet books provides all of your students chances to actively listen, look, think, and read. Using your students names in alphabet books enhances learning and makes making alphabet books even more enjoyable.

Predictable Charts with Names

Chapter 6

There is a special kind of shared writing that was once called "structured language experience" (Cunningham, 1979). We now call it "predictable charts." Language experience (Stauffer, 1970; Van Allen, 1964) is a writing approach to teaching reading. When using the language experience approach, teachers take dictation from individual children and help them learn to read their dictation. Language experience advocates believed that children would be able to read their dictation since it was their own language. Children would understand what was written because it was their own experiences. But what about the child that does not talk in complete sentences and therefore cannot dictate a complete sentence? These children could not usually read the sentence the teacher wrote because the sentence was not their language. Structured language experience, or predictable charts, allows children with limited oral language to participate in language experience.

In her article written in 1979, Pat Cunningham describes the structured language experience as a writing/reading approach in which the majority of children can take part in both saying and reading their own sentences. Teachers choose a predictable pattern to begin each sentence and write down what the children say. Children can then read back what the teacher writes.

How is this possible? This experience is possible if two things happen. First, the teacher must choose a topic children know about or are learning about. Second, the teacher must choose a structure for the children to follow when writing the class sentences (for example, I like to _.). When all the children in the class use the same structure for their dictated sentences, those who cannot make up sentences on their own can follow the pattern and find success.

Using the same sentence structure for each sentence on the chart helps all children in the class take part in the reading/writing experience without having to wait for further language development. Young children learn they can dictate a complete sentence following the chosen sentence pattern. They also learn that they are able to read the sentence back to the teacher and the class. To be successful, children simply follow the sentence structure used by the children reading the sentences before them.

When emergent readers read predictable books, books predictable by either pictures or print, they experience success. Structured Language Experience charts are similar to predictable books and so we call them predictable charts. Writing predictable charts helps emergent readers and writers experience success also. A predictable chart starts with a predictable pattern or structure: I see . . . , I like . . . , My friend is . . . , etc. Each sentence begins the same way on the chart. Children's names are often in parentheses after the dictated sentences, but sometimes children's names actually begin the sentences. In this chapter, you will find examples of predictable charts with children's names at both the end and the beginning of sentences. *Month-by-Month Reading, Writing, and Phonics for Kindergarten* (Hall and Cunningham, 2003) includes ideas for "easy" predictable charts beginning early in the year.

Some ideas for early in the year predictable charts include:

- After reading a predictable book, *Things I Like* by Anthony Browne (Bantam Doubleday Dell Books for Young Readers, 1997) you can have the children finish the sentence "I like to _."

- After reading *The Little Engine That Could* by Watty Piper (Grosset & Dunlap, 1976) you could have the children finish the sentence "I can _."

- After talking about colors and being introduced to color words, the predictable chart begins, "My favorite color is _." (Write the sentences with students' favorite color markers!)

- At Thanksgiving, after reading and talking about this special day, you can write a predictable chart, "I am thankful for _."

- After a field trip (to a farm, historical site, or a museum) a popular predictable chart is, "I saw a _."

For a whole book on predictable charts see *Predictable Charts* by Dorothy P. Hall and Elaine Williams (Carson-Dellosa, 2001).

Five Day Cycle for Predictable Charts

Ideas for predictable charts come from things that are happening in the classroom, at school, and outside school. Many teachers find a five-day cycle works well for each predictable chart made with the class.

Day 1 and Day 2: Dictation of the Sentences

Give students a model or a pattern to follow. The children dictate their sentences using the given model. Write each child's sentence on a large piece of chart paper and put the child's name in parentheses at the end. After the dictation of each sentence, let each child read her sentence back as you point to the words. Dictation and writing the chart often take one day for a small class (10-15 students) and two days for larger classes.

Day 3: Touch Reading and Matching Words

On the third day, ask each student to "touch read" his sentence on the chart. Moving the chart to the student's eye level makes reading easier. Touching each word helps children learn to track print. Sometimes you can ask the student to find the longest or shortest word in his sentence or talk about the capital letters and punctuation.

Once the class has done several charts and they all understand the process, children work on word order in their sentences. Give the children their cut-up sentences in clear sandwich bags. Then, call on two or three children to match their cut-up sentences to their written sentences on the predictable chart. After these children place the words in a pocket chart, have them compare the order of the cut-up words to the order of the written words on the chart. Once the class has seen this modeled by a student (sometimes with the teacher's help), they all arrange the words in their cut-up sentence to match their sentence on the predictable chart. While the children are doing this, walk around the room, monitor, help students who need it, and listen to the children read their sentences after matching them to the predictable chart.

Day 4: Sentence Builders

Today, focus on the sentence, the word, the sounds of letters, and the letters. Before the lesson, choose three sentences from the chart and write them on sentence strips. Include the name of the child who dictated the sentence. Cut the words apart and put them in an envelope or plastic bag ready to use. Use one sentence at a time and pass out the words to as many children as you have words, often giving the name to the child whose sentence the children are going to build. Then, ask students to be "sentence builders." This means students come up to the front of the room and get themselves in the right place in the sentence and show their words to the class. Some students know their words and can do this task quite easily. Other students have to match the words they are holding to the chart and count words to find their right places. Children often help each other find the right place for each word in the sentence. The child who is holding her name usually knows where to stand—at the end! Finally, stand behind the sentence builders and touch each child as you read the sentence with the class. Repeat this process for the other two cut-up sentences.

Once students are used to building sentences, begin to ask questions about the sentences— "Can you find a certain word? Can you find a word that starts like _? Can you find a word that rhymes with _? Can you find a word that begins with a certain letter?"

Day 5: Making a Class Book
Begin by letting each child read his sentence from the chart. Then, let the class read the chart story together with you. Give each child his cut-up sentence. (You will have to prepare these ahead of time!) The children put the words in the correct order and glue the words to the bottom of a page. Next, they will illustrate their sentences. Make a book cover and staple the book together. Now, the students have a class big book to treasure all year! As the year progresses, give the sentence strips to the students and let the students cut apart the words in their sentences. You may also mix up the words in the sentence so that students have to cut the words apart, as well as paste them in the right order. You can also let them copy or type their sentences for books. The more children learn, the more they are able to do successfully!

Predictable Charts with Names

At the beginning of this chapter we mentioned some of the popular, easy, predictable charts. One of the easiest charts to begin with is, "My name is _." Teachers usually start the year doing some get acquainted activities and learning the students' names. The teacher writes "Names" on the top of the chart. In the first sentence she tells her name:

My name is Mrs. Hall.

Then, the teacher calls on a student to tell what his name is. Steven says, "My name is Steven." The teacher writes the words as Steven says them. Next, the teacher calls on another student who answers, "My name is Patty." One by one, each child uses this model and completes the sentence with her name.

Days 1 and 2: Dictation of the Sentences

Talk about the names of the students in your class. Begin your predictable chart with the sentence, "My name is _." Finish this sentence the first time with your name. After writing your sentence first on the predictable chart, read it back to the class. Then, ask each student to tell you his sentence saying, "My name is" and completing the sentence with his name. As each child dictates his sentence, write it on the chart. Writing the chart will take one day and sometimes two days when you have a large class.

Day 3: Touch Reading and Matching Words

On the third day, ask each student to "touch read" her sentence on the chart. Each child reads, "My name is" and says her name. Together with the class, start at the top of the chart and read to the bottom. Each child takes a turn. If you have children that need a little extra help do not call on them at the beginning. After a few sentences, they pick up the pattern and can be successful at this task.

Day 4: Sentence Builders

On Day 4, focus on the sentence, the word, the sounds of letters, and the letters. Before the lesson, write three sentences from the chart on three sentence strips; the name of each child who dictated each sentence is included in these sentences. Cut apart the words and put them in three envelopes or plastic bags ready for use in class. Use one sentence at a time and pass out the words to four children, making sure to give the name to the child whose sentence it is. Students are then asked to be "sentence builders." To do this correctly, the child holding "My" has to get at the beginning of the sentence. The next place in line belongs to the child holding "name." In the third place is the child holding the word "is." The last spot belongs to the child holding her name. Finally, stand behind the "sentence builders" and touch each child as you read the sentence with the class. Repeat this process for the other two cut-up sentences.

Day 5: Making a Class Book

On Day 5, if you think your children can handle this task, then for this predictable chart write the sentences from the chart on drawing paper and let the children add their handwritten name to the sentence, "My name is _." Children do not have to put the words in the correct order and glue them to the bottom of a page; all they have to do is illustrate their sentences once they have written their names. To finish the book, make a front cover (with title), a back cover (plain), and staple the pages inside in the order they appear on the chart. Now the students have a class big book with all the names of the students in their class. Some primary students will be able to read each sentence including the names of all the students. Other children will be able to read just their sentences. Still others pick up the book and search for the pages they did and look for their names because these are the first words they can read. This class big book, written by the children and including all of their names and self-portraits, is a wonderful addition to any primary classroom's reading center!

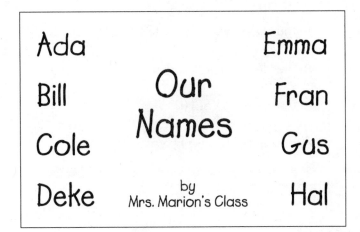

Arthur Predictable Chart

There are many books about Arthur the aardvark, who acts (and looks) more human than aardvark! These books can be a catalyst to writing a predictable chart. After reading several *Arthur* books (for example, *Arthur Writes a Story* by Marc Brown (Little, Brown Children's Books, 1998) you can begin a predictable chart about Arthur.

Arthur the Aardvark

Arthur likes to write. (Mrs. Hall)

Arthur likes computers. (Ryan)

Arthur likes D.J. (Michelle)

Arthur likes vacations. (Zannie)

Arthur likes to walk. (Karen)

Arthur likes hikes. (Dan)

Arthur likes to exercise. (Missy)

Ira Sleeps Over Predictable Chart

Another favorite book for primary children is *Ira Sleeps Over* by Bernard Waber (Houghton Mifflin Co., 1973). It is the story of a young boy asked to sleep over at his friends house. Ira, the young boy, worries how will he make it without his nighttime companion—his bear. This leads to a class discussion of sleepovers. Some children know quite a lot about them; others can just imagine what it is to sleep away from mom, dad, teddy or "blankie." The question is asked at the end of the discussion, "What do you do at a sleepover?" The teacher and the class together write a predictable chart and a list of things they could do at a sleepover. For this names chart, we will start with the name of the student and write what they said they would do.

What Do You Like to Do at a
Sleepover?

Mrs. Cunningham likes to read stories.

David likes to tell stories.

Kathleen likes to eat popcorn.

José likes to watch movies.

Matthew likes to play video games.

Kristen likes to stay up until midnight.

Days 1 and 2: Dictation of the Sentences

Read the book and talk about sleepovers with your class. (Have you ever slept over at some-body's house? What did you do? What did you take with you? Where did you sleep? Were you scared?) If you have a large class, more than 15 students, begin the sentence dictation and writing of the chart on the first day and finish this task on the second day. If you have a small number of students (lucky you!) you can read and discuss the first day and have the children dictate their sentences the second day.

Day 3: Touch Reading the Sentences and Matching

On the third day, ask each student to "touch read" his sentence on the chart. Let children use a special pointer with a gold star at the end to point to the words as they read their sentences. Tell students to pretend they are reading at night by starlight! (What fun!) Each child reads, "_likes to __." and tells how he finished the sentence. Together with the class, start at the top of the chart and read to the bottom. Each child takes a turn. If you know that some children need a little extra help, do not call on them at the beginning; wait until near the end. After a few sentences, most children can pick up the pattern and be successful.

Day 4: Sentence Builders

Today, focus on the sentence, the word, the sounds of letters, and the letters. Before the lesson write three sentences from the chart on three sentence strips. (The names of the children who dictated these sentences begin these sentences.) Cut apart the words and put them in an envelope or plastic bag ready to use in class. Use one sentence at a time and pass out the words to some children, making sure to give the name to the child whose sentence it is. Then, ask students to be "sentence builders." Finally, stand behind the "sentence builders" and touch each child as you read the sentence with the class. Repeat this process for the other two cut-up sentences.

Day 5: Making a Class Book

Each child gets her own sentence. The words for their sentences are cut apart. Next, children put the words in the correct order, you check the sentences, and then they glue the words at the bottom of their pages. When the sentence is correctly glued at the bottom of the page, each child illustrates her sentence. To finish the book, make a front cover (with the title, "What You Do at a Sleepover") and a back cover (plain), then staple the pages inside in the order they appear on the chart. Now students have another class book to put in the reading center or to read another day while having a "pretend sleepover" with your class!

Gregory, the Terrible Eater Predictable Chart

A good book to read during a health unit is *Gregory, the Terrible Eater* by Mitchell Sharmat (Scholastic, Inc., 1983). This book can lead to a class discussion of some foods that are good for you and some foods that are not good for you. Bringing in samples of good food for the children to taste can add to the discussion but is not necessary. After your discussion, begin a predictable chart about good food the children like to eat. The chart can be titled, "Good Food" or "We Are Not Like Gregory, We Like To Eat." You can begin each sentence with the child's name and then write what they said they liked to eat.

This is what a finished chart may look like:

> **We are NOT like Gregory,**
> **We Like to Eat**
>
> Mrs. Hall likes to eat cheese.
>
> Suzanne like to eat pizza.
>
> Chris likes to eat watermelon.
>
> Ryan likes to eat apples.
>
> Zannie likes to eat grapes.
>
> Kristen likes to eat chicken.
>
> Julie likes to eat bananas.

Day 1 and 2: Dictation and Writing the Sentences

Read the book *Gregory, the Terrible Eater*. You might bring in some of your favorite healthy foods (little carrots, tender celery, dry roasted peanuts, fresh strawberries, etc.) or ask the parents of your students if they could send their favorite healthy snack to school. Cut the fresh fruits and vegetables in small pieces for a tasting party. Talk about students' favorite healthy foods, not foods that are too sugary or fast foods. If any child says french fries or candy is a favorite food, remind her that those foods are not nutritious; they have too much sugar or too much fat.

Day 3: Touch Reading the Sentences and Matching

On the third day, let each student "touch read" his sentence on the chart. Each child starts with his name and then reads what healthy food he said he liked to eat to finish the sentence. Together with the class, start at the top of the chart and read to the bottom. Each child takes a turn. If you know that some children need a little extra help, do not call on them at the beginning for dictation; wait until near the end. After a few sentences, most children can pick up the pattern and be successful both in dictation and in "touch reading" their sentences.

Day 4: Sentence Builders

Today, focus on the sentence, the word, the sounds of letters, and the letters. Before the lesson, write three sentences from the chart on three sentence strips. (The name of each child who dictated a sentence begins his sentence.) Cut apart the words and put them in an envelope or plastic bag ready to use in class. Use one sentence at a time and pass out the words to children, making sure to give the name to the child whose sentence it is. Then, ask students to be "sentence builders." Finally, stand behind the "sentence builders" and touch each child as you read the sentence with the class. Repeat this process for the other two cut-up sentences.

Day 5: Making a Class Book

Each child gets her own sentence. The words for children's sentences are cut apart. Next, children put the words in the correct order, you check the sentences, and then they glue the words at the bottom of their pages. When the sentence is correctly glued at the bottom of the page, each child illustrates her sentence. To finish the book, make a front cover (with the title, "Good Food") and a back cover (plain), then staple the pages inside in the order they appear on the chart. Now, students have another class book to put in the reading center.

Other Ideas

People and Places

Mrs. Hall went to Lake of the Ozarks.

Ryan went to Daytona.

Kathleen went to Rhode Island.

David went to San Diego.

Zannie went to Orlando.

There are many ideas for predictable charts with names. When talking about places the children went or will go during break or summer vacation, you could make a predictable chart.

How Many Letters in Our Names

Suzanne has 7 letters.

Ryan has 4 letters.

Julie has 5 letters.

Michelle has 8 letters.

When counting letters in the children's names for a math activity (see Chapter 13, page 124,) you could make a predictable chart with the children's names and the number of letters in them.

Predictable charts are ideal shared writing experiences—the sentences follow a pattern and children's names are always involved. Ideas for making predictable charts are endless!

Interactive Charts with Names

Chapter 7

Interactive charts, like predictable charts, provide patterns for children to follow. Both kinds of charts help children become better readers and writers. Interactive charts provide children an opportunity to manipulate text and interact with print as they learn to read text. An interactive chart can be based on a nursery rhyme, a familiar song or poem, finger play, or topic your class is studying. As emergent readers, young children are active, concrete learners who need a lot of support. Interactive charts based on easy-to-learn rhymes, poems, songs, or verses help young children quickly learn to "read" the words with little effort.

Interactive charts also help transfer oral language skills to written language skills. The charts help children begin to match oral words with written text. They provide children with the opportunity to learn to self-check and self-correct, or "cross check." As children read these interactive charts, they gain control over printed words and develop an "I can read" attitude.

After the children become more familiar with names and print in kindergarten, teachers often use the Getting to Know You chart (Chapter 1, page 10) early in the first and second grade years. Teachers usually begin the year with some get-acquainted activities. Getting to Know You is a name activity where the children learn about their classmates. The teacher focuses on a special child each day. Looking at a different name each day, emergent readers learn letter names, print concepts, and letter-sounds while learning about their classmates. Once the class has completed the Getting to Know You activity with the children's first names, they can do the activity a second time with an interactive chart.

You can make your own Getting to Know You interactive chart or use the commercially made chart. (See the "Getting to Know You Chart" in the *Building Blocks "Plus" for Kindergarten Bulletin Board* set from Carson-Dellosa.)

First, write the following sentence starters on sentence strips:

My name is _.

I am _ years old.

My favorite color is _.

I like to eat _.

I like to play _.

Next, on separate sentence strips, write words that fit the blanks in the sentence starters. (You know the most popular answers for all of the sentences from the first round when the children did this orally.)

- Write all of the **children's names** for the first sentence.

- Write **4, 5, 6,** or **7** for the answers to the second sentence.

- Write **red, yellow, blue, green, orange, purple, brown, white, pink,** and **black** for the answers for the third sentence on the interactive chart, and then put the color above the word with crayon or colored marker. This will help some children to "read" the color words.

- Write **pizza, hamburgers, tacos, grilled cheese sandwiches,** etc., for the fourth sentence (whatever most of the children said the first time around in Getting to Know You) and draw a picture above each word to help the children "read" these words and select the right one.

- For the final sentence, write the things most children said that they liked to do and draw a picture to help some children "read" these words (for example, **football, soccer, basket-ball, Nintendo®, computer games,** etc.).

Then, place the sentences starters in the pocket chart.

Finally, place the words the children will choose for each line after each of the sentences.

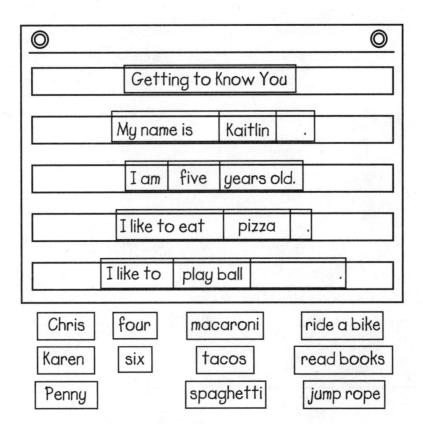

The first reading of an interactive chart is just for children to listen and enjoy. Model reading one child's name and the answers that complete the sentences for that child. Next, you and the class read that child's chart together. The third reading of this interactive chart is generally done by the child who gave the answers on the chart. Repeated reading of the chart helps young children remember the words and match oral words to written text. Once young children know letters and letter sounds, it gives them an opportunity to self-check words and self-correct.

Each day, interview the special student of the day who completes the five sentences by choosing one of the interactive pieces. First, the student of the day shares her name and her age. Then, she tells the class about her favorite food, and finally a word or two about what she likes to do. As children find the words to complete each sentence, read the sentence back to the class. This may be done in a pocket chart and rewritten on chart paper so that children can illustrate their sentences and the chart can be displayed on a bulletin board or wall. Children are proud and usually after a few readings they can read their own charts to family members and friends.

Interactive charts can be placed around the room (for reading the room) or in a reading center for the children to read independently at center time. There are lots of ideas for interactive charts made for books you read and themes you study all year long. Here are some ideas to get you started.

Nursery Rhyme Interactive Charts
Preparation:

- Read nursery rhymes with names during a teacher read-aloud to your class.

- Choose a favorite nursery rhyme with a name and make the chart using either lined paper or sentence strips and a pocket chart. Names are chosen for blanks in the sentences on the chart. The chart uses index cards for names of children in the class. Let the children choose their names and read the chart.

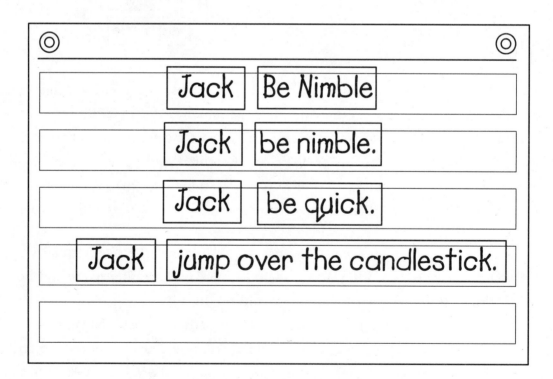

(Use children's names in place of Jack.)

Steps:

1. Introduce the chart to students during "big group" time.

2. Read the original nursery rhyme several times.

3. Choose five names of children in the class and have three copies of each chosen name ready. Model how to place the chosen name cards to fill in the missing parts in the first, second, and third lines. Then, read the new rhyme to and with the class.

4. Repeat with the other names until the children can easily read the rhyme. Have fun!

5. Place the interactive chart in the reading center, along with name cards for each student.

Examples:

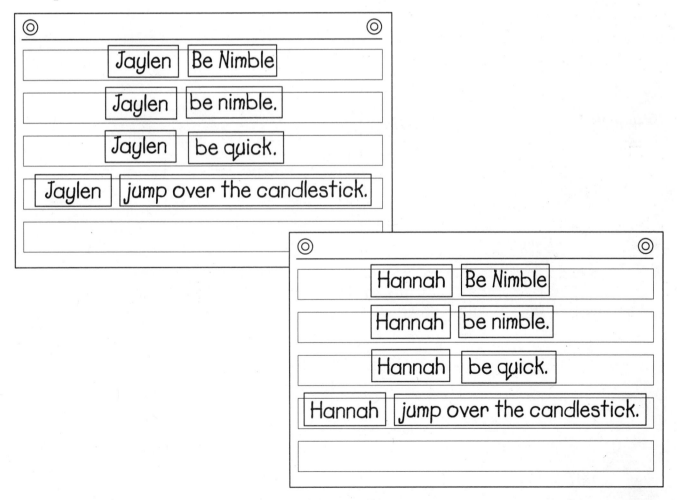

You can do the same with other nursery rhymes like:

Chart:

Use children's names
in place of Johnny.

Examples:

 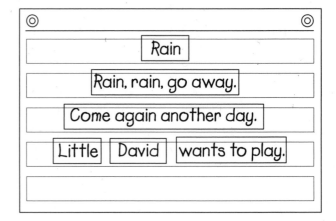

Chart:

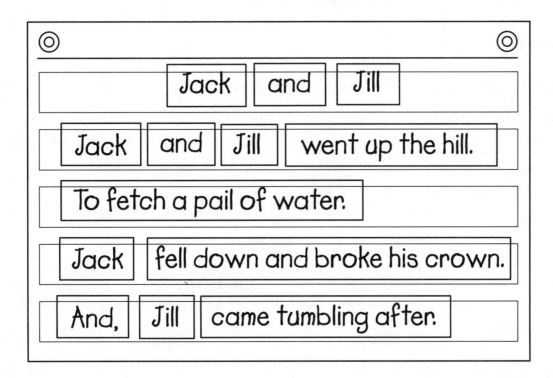

Examples:

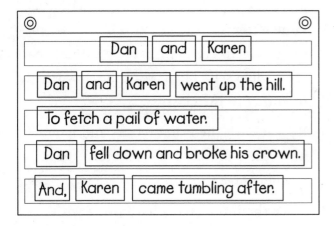

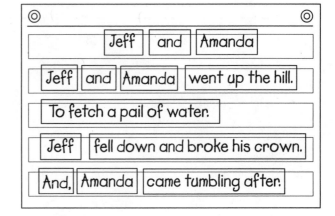

"A, My Name Is . . ." Interactive Chart

Preparation:

- Read the book during a teacher read-aloud to your class.

- Make the "A, My Name Is . . ." chart using either lined paper or sentence strips and a pocket chart. Words are chosen for each letter and written on cards. This chart can be used to review letter sounds at the end of the year with your students. The chart uses cards for letters, names, places, and things to sell.

Chart:

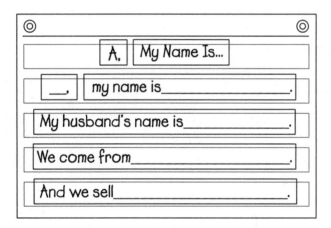

Steps:

1. Introduce the chart to students during "big group" time.

2. Read the original rhyme several times.

3. Model how to replace the letter in the rhyme with another letter and then find a girl's name and boy's name to fill in the missing parts in the first two lines. Find a place and a product, that begin with that same letter, for the last two lines. Use pictures to help children name products that the people sell. Then, read the new rhyme to and with the class.

4. Repeat with the other letters and names until the children can easily read the rhyme. Have fun!

5. Place the interactive chart along with word cards for each letter in the reading center.

Examples:

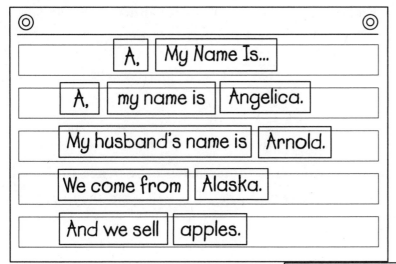

A, My Name Is...

A, my name is Angelica.

My husband's name is Arnold.

We come from Alaska.

And we sell apples.

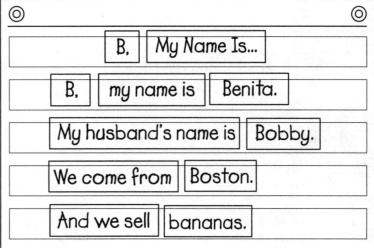

B, My Name Is...

B, my name is Benita.

My husband's name is Bobby.

We come from Boston.

And we sell bananas.

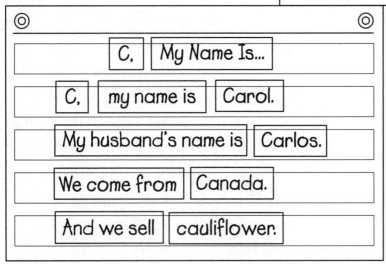

C, My Name Is...

C, my name is Carol.

My husband's name is Carlos.

We come from Canada.

And we sell cauliflower.

Interactive Charts with Traditional Rhymes or Songs

There are many rhymes and songs, some old and some new, with names. Think of the rhymes you used to jump rope to on the playground of old. Here are two old favorites; the first is found in many basal readers and songbooks for young readers.

Preparation:

- Introduce your students to the rhyme or song. Help them become familiar with it.

- Make the "Mary Wore Her Red Dress" chart using either lined paper or sentence strips and a pocket chart. Words are chosen for each name and what they will wear, then written on cards.

Chart:

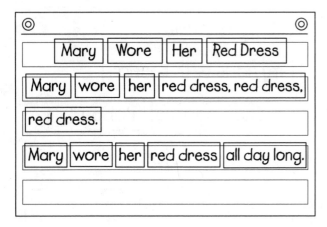

Steps:

1. Introduce the chart to the students during "big group" time.

2. Choose one student's name and have him say what he wants to wear to complete the chart.

3. Read the completed chart to the children several times.

4. Model how to replace missing parts (name and an article to wear) in the two lines of the song. You will have to write his name before the color and article of clothing he chooses. Then, read the new sentences to and with the class. Have fun! You can let each child use his name and an article of clothing he likes to wear; also let him choose a color and whether to write his or her. Do this over and over until all children have had their turns.

5. Place the interactive chart along with word cards for each child and what they choose to wear in the reading center.

Examples:

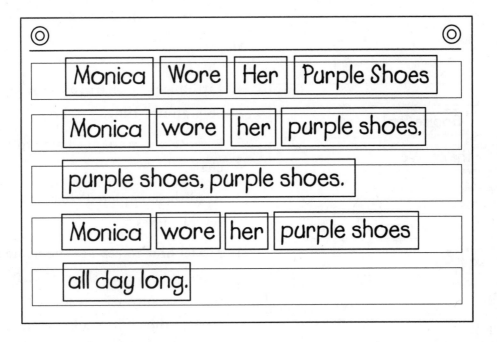

Monica | Wore | Her | Purple Shoes

Monica | wore | her | purple shoes,

purple shoes, purple shoes.

Monica | wore | her | purple shoes

all day long.

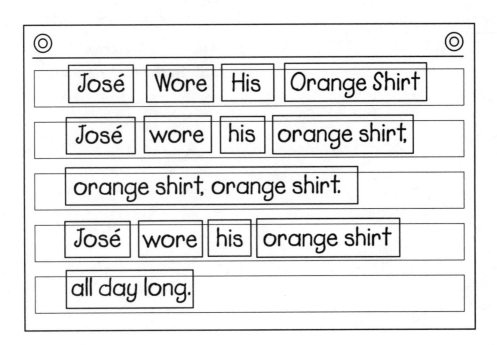

José | Wore | His | Orange Shirt

José | wore | his | orange shirt,

orange shirt, orange shirt.

José | wore | his | orange shirt

all day long.

Here is another song most teachers know; this one is even more fun because it can be read in parts.

Chart:

Cookie Jar

Who stole the cookie

from the cookie jar?

Michael | stole the cookie from the

cookie jar.

Who me?

Yes, you!

Not I.

Then who?

Steps:

1. Introduce the chart to the students during "big group" time.

2. Choose one student's name to complete the chart.

3. Read the completed chart to the children several times.

4. Model how to replace the name in each sentence. Then, read the new chart to and with the class. Alternate reading lines with the class or the child whose name is on the line. Have fun! You can let each child use her name and do this chart over and over again until all children have had their turns.

5. Place the interactive chart along with name cards in the reading center.

Examples:

Cookie Jar	
Who stole the cookie	(Read together.)
from the cookie jar?	
Michael stole the cookie	(Teacher reads.)
from the cookie jar.	
Who me?	(Child reads.)
Yes, you!	(Teacher reads.)
Not I.	(Child reads.)
Then who?	(Teacher reads.)

Cookie Jar	
Who stole the cookie	(Read together.)
from the cookie jar?	
Emily stole the cookie	(Teacher reads.)
from the cookie jar.	
Who me?	(Child reads.)
Yes, you!	(Teacher reads.)
Not I.	(Child reads.)
Then who?	(Teacher reads.)

Book Characters Interactive Charts

Here is an interactive chart you can make that uses the names of book characters. Once a book character is chosen, the children have only one choice for each line that follows. After reading Chapter 11 (pages 108-121) you may be able to think of other characters to use in interactive charts.

Preparation:

- Read the books during teacher read-alouds to your class.
- Make the Book Characters chart using either lined paper or sentence strips and a pocket chart. Children choose the words to fill in the blanks in the sentences on the chart. The chart uses cards for characters, the animals they are, descriptive words, and other characters they meet in the books.

Chart:

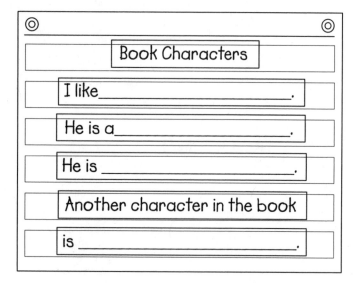

Words to make: Curious George, Clifford, Franklin, Arthur

Words to make: monkey, dog, turtle, aardvark

Words to make: big and red, brown and curious, always afraid, an aardvark

Words to make: the man with the yellow hat, Emily, D.J., anyone who helps

Steps:

1. Introduce the chart to the students during "big group" time.

2. Choose one book character and complete the chart.

3. Read the completed chart to the children several times.

4. Model how to replace missing parts in the four lines with another character, words to describe that character, and another character in the same book. Then, read the new chart to and with the class. Have fun!

5. Place the interactive chart along with word cards for each of the four blanks in the sentences in the reading center.

Examples:

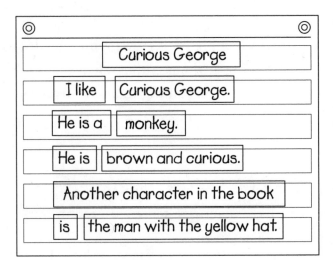

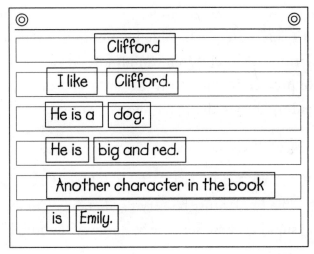

Once you have made an interactive chart and taught children during a big group or reading lesson how to use and read it, you can move the chart into the reading center. Here, children can manipulate the word cards in the interactive chart and read for independent practice. Children enjoy interactive charts, especially those with their names or the names of favorites characters.

Shared Reading with Names Books

Chapter 8

Shared reading is a wonderful way to expose emergent readers to books and print. Shared reading can be done with big books, teacher-made, and store-bought charts. When a child sits on a mother's or caregiver's lap, he sees both the pictures and the print. Children who have been read to from an early age know a lot about books from observing both the pictures and the print. Shared reading with big books can also provide these experiences for the children who have not been so fortunate at home. What the teacher does before and after reading a big book can move children forward in their literacy learning. The best books for the youngest readers are predictable by pictures or repetitive print. When big books are predictable by pictures, then children can almost "read the words" by looking at the picture. When big books are predictable by print, the children hear the pattern and are soon joining in and sharing the reading, hence the name shared reading.

What to Look for When Choosing a Big Book for Shared Reading

1. The book must be very predictable. The book must have repetitive sentences, pictures to support these sentences, and not too much print on each page.

2. Since the entire class will work with the same big book, the book should be enjoyable and appealing to most of the children.

3. The book must be able to "take students someplace" conceptually. Most teachers spend a week or two with a book—reading, rereading, acting out the story, and building connections to the theme or unit to extend the children's knowledge.
(Hall and Cunningham, 1997, 2003)

With a shared reading lesson as with any reading lesson, there is a before-reading stage, a during-reading stage, and an after-reading stage. In the **before-reading** part, the teacher builds prior knowledge and gets ready to read the story by talking about experiences related to the book. The teacher talks about some new or important words in the book—words that children need to know to be able to read and understand the book. The teacher will also tell children what they will do after the story, so children can focus on what they need to be successful in the after-reading activity.

The **during-reading** part of the lesson involves the teacher reading the big book to the children first, and then the children joining in and sharing the reading the second time. Echo, choral, or shared reading may be part of the during-reading stage. Pointing to the words as they are read then helps children focus on both the repetition of sound and print. During subsequent readings, children will be asked to "read it again" for a different purpose and do more of the reading.

In the **after-reading** part of the lesson, the teacher focuses on comprehension and understanding by leading a discussion and/or asking questions. If it is a story, the teacher may ask about the characters, setting, and what happened at the beginning, middle, and end. The teacher may ask who, what, where, when, and why questions. The teacher may also ask, "How do you know that?" The class might be asked to draw pictures about the story or their favorite part of the story, or to act out the story. Sometimes the teacher tosses a beach ball with story questions written on each stripe. After reading is also a time to talk about words (long words, short words, rhyming words, high-frequency words, etc.) or letter sounds that might help children figure out new words in other books.

Shared Reading with Big Books with Names in the Titles

Here are some big books with names in the titles that are good books for shared reading. In the primary grades, many teachers like to spend a week or two on a book. Other teachers spend a day or two on a big book, but that does not give much time for rereading which is essential to building fluency.

The Little Red Hen retold by Janina Domanska

(Houghton Mifflin Co., 1991; Macmillan, Inc., 1973)

In this retelling of the story the Little Red Hen finds a grain of wheat. The cat, rat, and goose will not help her plant the wheat, nor cut the wheat, nor take it to the mill. They would not help her carry the flour home from the mill, nor bake the bread. But, when it came time to eat the bread the cat, rat, and goose are ready to help!

Day One

Before: Have a cover talk with students. "Who is on the cover? What is she doing? Can you find the word Little? Red? Hen? Can you see the author's name? Let's read it together." Then, take a picture walk through the book talking about what is happening on each page. Talk about some words—the vocabulary on page 6, "grain" and "wheat;" page 8, "plant;" page 10, "buried;" page 14, "cut" and "thresh;" page 18, "threshed" and "wing;" page 22, "carried;" page 28, "baked." Use the picture and text to help figure out these words with the children. Tell the children that after you read you will discuss what happened and toss the beach ball with the story questions on it.

During: "Listen to the story and see if we were right when we told the story using the pictures." Read the book to the children. When you are finished reading ask, "Were we right?"

"I am going to read the story again, this time you can join and help me read the story."

After: Toss the beach ball to the children and let them discuss what happened in the story after reading each stripe.

Day Two

Before: Use the pictures to retell the story. "Today, after we read the book and you will read after me, then we are going to make a list of all of the things Little Red Hen did."

During: Echo reading—read a page and then have the children be your echo and read the page after you.

After: Make a list of all of the things Little Red Hen did.

Little Red Hen found a grain of wheat.

She buried the wheat in the ground.

She cut the wheat with her bill.

She threshed the wheat with her

   wings.

She carried the wheat to the mill.

She carried the flour home.

She made the bread and baked it.

(You can read the book once more to see if you are right.)

Day Three

Before: Talk about the characters. "Who do you think was the worker? Which characters were lazy? What character would you like to be? Can everyone be Little Red Hen?"

During: "Do the book." Assign the parts to the children (hen, cat, dog, goose, chicks). Read the book two or three times with different children taking the different parts.

After: Let each child draw his favorite part of the story.

(There is another big book version retold by Brenda Parks available from Rigby, 1984.)

Moonbear's Books **by Frank Asche**

(Houghton Mifflin School Division, 1993; Simon and Schuster, 1993)

This book is about a bear that likes books!

Day One

Before: Cover talk and picture walk. Discuss the pictures on the cover of the book and what is happening in the book. Use the pictures and print to figure out the kinds of books Moonbear likes.

During: Read aloud the book to the children. Then, read it again and let the children join in and share the reading. As you start, remind them to use the pictures to help them.

After: Discuss the book. "What kinds of books did Moonbear like to read?" Write the books Moonbear likes to read on sentence strips and place them in a pocket chart.

Day Two

Before: Go over the list books that Moonbear liked.

During: Do an echo reading of each page. After reading each page, check to see if that book is on the list you made with the class.

After: Start a predictable chart of the different kinds of books that you and the children like.

What Kind of Books Do YOU Like?

I like alphabet books. (Mrs. Hall)

I like Dr. Seuss books. (Michelle)

I like race car books. (Ryan)

I like cat books. (Kathleen)

I like picture books. (Suzanne)

I like surfing books. (David)

I like Berenstain Bear books. (Zannie)

Day Three

Before: Talk about the books Moonbear likes and the list you started yesterday.

During: Have a shared reading of the book and then read the list you started. Help each child "touch read" her sentence. Then, finish the predictable chart by writing down the rest of the students' dictated sentences.

After: Give each child their sentence on a sentence strip and have them cut the words apart. Then, have children paste their sentences on large, 18" x 24" manila drawing paper and illustrate their sentences. Make a class big book from the sentences by stapling the papers together.

Hattie and the Fox **by Mem Fox**

(DC Heath Company, 1989; Macmillan, 1987)

In this book, Hattie, a big black hen notices something in the bushes:

"Goodness gracious me!

I can see a nose in the bushes!"

The other animals respond:

"Good grief," said the goose.

"Well, well," said the pig.

"Who cares?" said the sheep.

"So what?" said the horse.

"What next?" said the cow.

As the story continues, Hattie sees a nose and two eyes in the bushes, then a nose, two eyes and two ears. Next two legs appear, followed by a body and two more legs. As Hattie announces each new sighting, the other animals respond with the same lack of concern.

But when Hattie announces it is a fox, the other animals respond:

"Oh, no!" said the goose.

"Dear me!" said the pig.

"Oh, dear!" said the sheep.

"Oh, help!" said the horse.

But the cow said "MOO!"

This frightens the fox away and the animals go on about their business.

Day One

Before: Do a cover talk and picture walk. Talk about the picture on the cover of the book and then take a picture walk through the book figuring out the names of the animals using both the pictures and print.

During: Teacher read aloud; as with any book, the first reading of a big book should be strictly focused on the meaning and enjoyment of the book. This book has delightful illustrations and children will enjoy the suspense of watching the fox emerge. Read it again and encourage children to join in. For this book, children will almost naturally want to say the repeated responses of the animals and join Hattie in adding the body parts as she sees them.

After: Talk about the animals in this book and what each animal said and repeated.

Day Two

Before: Review the story using the pictures on each page as a catalyst. Tell the students that after you echo read this story you will toss the beach ball so pay attention to the characters, setting, and what happened in the beginning, middle, and end of this story.

During: Echo read the book by reading each line and then having children be your echo and reading it again.

After: Toss the beach ball to children and have them answer the questions on the stripes.

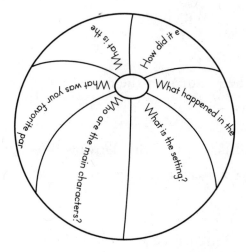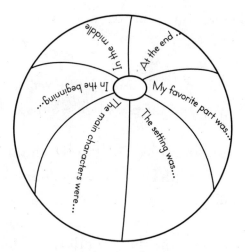

Day Three

Before: To review the story with the class, fill out a story map with characters, setting, beginning, middle, and end.

During: Read the story again. This time choose children to read the various parts, including a storyteller to read the lines that don't belong to animals and are not repetitive. You may want to do this if your class has not done this before.

After: "Act it Out"—Young children are natural actors. They pretend and act out all kinds of things. Choose another set of characters; let them put on yarned necklaces with a simple drawing of the main characters so everyone will know who they are! Let the children act it out several times so that everyone has a chance to be one of the animals. You can read the part that is not repetitive and let children in the audience read with you.

***Annie, Bea, and Chi Chi Delores: A School Day Alphabet Book* by Donna Maurer**
(Houghton Mifflin School Division, 1996; Orchard Books, 1993)
All aboard this alphabet book for a trip through the alphabet at school. Each letter takes you on another adventure at school until you zip your jacket and go home.

Day One
Before: Do a cover talk and picture walk. Talk about the pictures on the cover and let the pictures help you and the class figure out some new words.

During: Read the book aloud to the children. Let children predict what letter will be next and what might be found at school beginning with that letter. Read this easy alphabet book again and let children join in and share the reading.

After: Talk about the things in this alphabet book that students see at school. Find the action words in the alphabet book and make a list of them. Let the children "do" the words.

Day Two
Before: Review the things in this book that students do at school.

During: Echo read and check their list of action words as you read the book. Do you need to add to the list?

After: Start an A-B-C list of things in your classroom.

***Cookie's Week* by Cindy Ward**
(Scholastic Big Books, 1988)
Each day of the week, a lovable cat finds a new place and a new way to get into trouble.

Day One
Before: Do a cover talk and picture walk. Ask, "Do you have a pet? Does it ever get into trouble?"

During: Read to the children, then do a shared reading of the book.

After: Talk about the days of the week and what happened to Cookie.

Day Two

Before: Retell the story by taking a picture walk through the big book.

During: Echo read the book with the class

After: In a pocket chart, sequence the days of the week written on index cards.

Day Three

Before: Begin a chart with two columns: "Day of the Week" and "Where Cookie Is."

During: Do a shared reading to check the chart and get ready to do a final column about what happened to Cookie.

After: Fill in the third column—"What Happened to Cookie."

***Rosie's Walk* by Pat Hutchins**

(Simon and Schuster, 1968)

A wonderful book to follow Rosie, a hen, and to review over, under, around, and other directional words.

Day One

Before: Do a cover talk and picture walk with the class.

During: Read the book to the children and then do a shared reading of it.

After: Make a list of the places Rosie walked, and talk about directional words.

Day Two

Before: Make a list of the directional words and see if the children can add where this happened. (over _, under _, around _, etc.)

During: Echo read the book to check the list.

After: Let the children write and draw their favorite places Rosie went.

Shared Reading of "Getting to Know You" Names Charts

Another activity we do with "Getting to Know You" names chart (page 10) is a shared reading of each child's chart. This can take place after writing it or later in the day and does not take more than twenty minutes. On the first day, you will only have one chart to read. Lead the children to read it chorally several times and let volunteers come and read each sentence. Guide their hands so that they are tracking print as they read. Most teachers display each chart for five days, and then let the child take her chart home, with instructions to display it on her bedroom door. That way, there are only five charts in the room at any one time but every chart gets read and reread on five different days.

Many teachers also write (or type) the article from the chart, and after all of the children have had their special days and been interviewed, compile a class book containing each article (often along with a picture of each child). Each child then has one night to take the book home so that his family can get to know the whole class.

Don't miss the opportunity to read and reread the "Getting to Know You" names charts. The names of the children and the repetition of sentences makes this a favorite first reading activity. There are many wonderful predictable big books teachers use for shared reading. Some of the big books have names in the title and provide teachers with other activities that focus on names. What teachers do before and after reading big books can help children move forward in their literacy learning. The during part of big books, or the reading and rereading, helps children develop fluency.

Using Environmental Print Names

Chapter 9

Most of the activities in this book have used the names of "important people" to anchor the concepts being taught. Since children are very egocentric, we always begin with their names and the names of important people in their environment to build new concepts. Once we have used their names in a variety of activities, however, we "branch out" and use the names of important things and places in their environments to continue to build and review concepts.

Building Letter-Sound Concepts with Environmental Print

Food is of universal interest to children and even three- and four-year olds can often read the names of their favorite cereals and treats. During a Foods unit, you might bring in packages of some popular cereals such as Cheerios®, Apple Jacks®, Froot Loops®, corn flakes, and Lucky Charms®. Display the packages and have the children talk about which ones they like—or don't like. You may want to review graphing skills by making a graph of your children's favorite cereals.

Once you have let students talk about the cereals, draw their attention to the names. Which cereal names take two words and which only take one? Which names have the most letters? The least? What letters on the boxes can they name? You can ask the children what they notice about the sounds of the letters. Perhaps someone will notice that Cheerios® and Charms start with **ch** and have the same sound. Corn starts with just a **c** and has the same sound as **cat**. Maybe they will notice that all of the cereals end with the letter **s**. The **s** at the end of corn flakes, Apple Jacks®, and Froot Loops® has an "**s**" sound, but the **s** at the end of Cheerios® and Lucky Charms® has a "**z**" sound.

Most young children are fascinated with the names of their favorite cereals and love noticing things about them. When they have made these discoveries for themselves, they are not apt to forget them. Often, students begin to notice letter sound patterns in words without our help and come tell us of their discoveries. If you give them a homework assignment to look at the foods they eat for breakfast and bring in their discoveries, you can increase the number of discoveries they make. You might want them to bring in empty packages or copy the names of the foods they make discoveries about. Let children share what they noticed and then encourage them to go home and discover something else. Here are some of the breakfast food discoveries some children made

Pop-Tarts® have an **s** and the "**s**" sound at the end.

Eggo® has the word **egg** in it.

Blueberry tarts and strawberry jelly both have the word **berry**.

Grape juice and granola start with **gr**.

Once you have exhausted the possibilities of breakfast foods, you can begin the process over again with some other names important to their world. Bring in menus, bags, or ads from some of their favorite eating places—McDonald's®, Burger King®, Taco Bell®, Pizza Hut®, Subway®. Again, let them talk about these places and what they like to eat there. You may once again want to graph their favorites because children, like adults, like knowing their opinions matter. Once they have had a chance to share their ideas about these restaurants, draw their attention to the words and letters. Help them notice and learn whatever there is to learn. Again, send them home with a homework assignment to bring in a menu or ad, or ask them to write the name of a favorite restaurant. Have children share what they noticed about the words, letters, and sounds.

You are probably thinking that this could go on forever and you are right! The homes and neighborhoods of some children, unfortunately, lack books, magazines, and newspapers but no child lives in a printless world! All children see words—product names, place names, signs—in their world every day. Once we draw their attention to this environmental print, it can become the source for them to discover and practice many important beginning reading concepts.

Building Rhyme and Vowel Pattern Concepts with Environmental Print

Rhyme has a universal appeal and is often incorporated in advertising campaigns for that reason. Campaign buttons in the 1950s indicated the candidate of choice by proclaiming, "I like Ike." Car ads suggested to, "See the USA in your Chevrolet®!" It is no coincidence that McDonald's® spokesperson is named Ronald. Rhymes are often used to draw attention to products as in Snack Pack®, Slim Jim® and Shake 'N Bake®.

Rhyming patterns are one of the easiest ways for children to learn to decode and spell new words. Children who know the words **day** and **play** can be shown how these words help them read and spell rhyming words with the same pattern such as **way, May, gray, clay, stray** and **Jay**. We can use product names which children easily recognize to help children learn how the words they know can help them decode and spell lots of other rhyming words.

For the first lesson, you might begin with three products whose names rhyme: Snack Pack®, Slim Jim® and Shake 'N Bake®. By starting with these rhyming products, we can immediately make the point to students that words with the same spelling pattern usually rhyme. Here is an outline of how this first lesson might go.

1. Begin by displaying the products and letting students talk about them. Do they recognize them, eat them, like them, etc.?

2. Have students identify the names and write these names to head three columns on the board or chart. Once they are all written, help students notice that they rhyme and then underline the spelling patterns (for example, **-ack, -im, -ake**).

   Snack Pack®   Slim Jim®   Shake 'N Bake®

   Point out to students that many rhyming words have the same spelling pattern. The spelling pattern begins with the first vowel and goes to the end of the syllable.

3. Have students divide a piece of paper into three columns and head these with Snack Pack®, Slim Jim® and Shake 'N Bake®, underlining the spelling pattern in each.

4. Tell students that you are going to show them some words and that they should write them under the product with the same spelling pattern. Show them words which you have written on index cards. Let different students go to the board and write the words as everyone is writing them on their papers. Do not let students pronounce the words until they are written on the board. Help students pronounce the words by making them rhyme.

Here are some words to use with **-ack, -im,** and **-ake:**

back	dim	cake	take	rack
trim	track	Kim	Tim	snake

5. Explain to students that thinking of rhyming words can also help them spell. This time you will not show them the words but you will say words and they will have to decide which product they rhyme with and which spelling pattern to use. Here are some **-ack, -im,** and **-ake** words you might pronounce and have them spell:

black	swim	lake	flake	smack
skim	shack	quack	quake	brim

6. End the lesson by helping students verbalize that in English, words that rhyme often have the same spelling pattern. You can read and spell other words by using the pattern in the rhyming word.

   Once you have shown the children how these product names help them spell many short words, you can extend this lesson by having children figure out how to decode and spell some longer words with the same patterns.

   Here are some possible **-ack, -im,** and **-ake** words you might use:

victim	shortcake	paperback	horseback	unpack
flashback	denim	soundtrack	drawback	feedback
handshake	outback	snowflake	racetrack	bookrack

There are an infinite number of lessons you can do using various product and place names to help your children learn to use rhyming patterns to decode and spell. Here are just a few possibilities of names of products and places to get you started.

Products: Sprite®, Coke®, grape

One-syllable words to read:

ape   bite   poke   scrape   tape   quite   stroke   white   choke

One-syllable words to spell:

kite   spite   broke   smoke   spoke   shape   drape   joke   cape

Longer words:

campsite   provoke   escape   shipshape   unite   invite   reunite   landscape   polite   impolite

Restaurants: Taco Bell®, Burger King®, Pizza Hut®

One-syllable words to read:

fell   part   shut   bring   yell   sting   string   shell   sell   rut   quell   fling

One-syllable words to spell:

ring   spring   swell   wing   swing   smell   strut   glut   spell   well

Longer words:

haircut   misspell   something   hamstring   undercut   dumbbell   Mozart   shortcut   seashell   darling   inning   peanut   retell   outsmart

Products: ice cream, Cool Whip®

One-syllable words to read:

nice   team   steam   stream   slice   school   vice   skip   beam   drool

One-syllable words to spell:

gleam   twice   dream   clip   price   pool   spool   scream   grip   spice

Longer words:

mainstream   downstream   gossip   preschool   whirlpool   spaceship   partnership   sunbeam   overprice   turnip   carpool   friendship   tulip   equip

Products: Kool-Aid®, popcorn

One-syllable words to read:

horn   cop   raid   worn   drop   maid   prop   fool   shop   born

One-syllable words to spell:

torn   flop   braid   scorn   crop   thorn   tool   stool   paid   chop

Longer words:

mermaid lollipop workshop   unicorn newborn bridesmaid toadstool
unpaid   raindrop gumdrop   acorn afraid prepaid   nonstop

Products: KitKat®, Goldfish®

One-syllable words to read:

spit   split   that   grit   flat   dish   bold   spat   mold   rat

One-syllable words to spell:

slit   old   hold   wish   swish   quit   chat   hat   hit   brat

Longer words:

admit   profit   misfit   wildcat   credit   democrat   selfish   unselfish   acrobat
permit   visit outfit   combat   nonfat   catfish   starfish   billfold   blindfold

Products: candy canes, jelly beans, Mounds®, Almond Joy®

One-syllable words to read:

found   dean   bound   crane   Roy   hound   plane   pound   mean   Jean

One-syllable words to spell:

round   ground   sane   toy   sound   lean   clean   lane   boy   Jane

Longer words:

compound   surround   annoy   humane   inhumane   soybean   employ
decoy   around   insane   airplane   enjoy   destroy   rebound

Look in your cupboards, in the grocery store, and at places in your neighborhood to find an endless source of environmental print to help your children use rhyme to decode and spell words. To get you started hunting for the words that work for your students, here are some names we have found for the most common rhyming patterns.

-ace	Ace Hardware®	-each	Reach®
-ack	Snack Pack®	-eam	ice cream
-ade	lemonade	-ean	jelly beans
-aid	Band-Aid®, Kool-Aid®	-ear	Goodyear®
-ail	nail polish	-eat	Wheat Thins®
-ain	White Rain®	-ee	fat free
-air	hair spray	-eed	Speed Stick®
-ake	Shake 'N Bake®	-een	Green Giant®
-ale	ginger ale	-eer	Cheer®
-all	All®	-eet	Sweet 'N Low®
-am	Pam®	-ell	Taco Bell®
-an	Ban®	-est	Crest®
-and	Band-Aid®	-ew	Mountain Dew®
-ane	candy canes	-ice	ice cream
-ank	(Your Local) Bank	-ick	Speed Stick®
-ap	ginger snaps	-ide	Tide®
-ape	grape		
-are	Ace Hardware®		
-art	Wal-Mart®		
-at	fat free, KitKat®		
-ate	Colgate®		
-ay	hair spray, Ocean Spray®		

-ight	Right Guard®	-one	Coppertone®
-im	Slim Jim®	-ood	Goodyear®
-ime	lemon lime	-ool	Cool Whip®, Kool-Aid®
-in	Wheat Thins®	-oot	root beer
-ine	Pine-Sol®	-op	popcorn
-ing	Burger King®	-ope	Scope®
-ip	Cool Whip®	-ore	The Dollar Store®
-ipe	fudge stripes	-orn	popcorn
-ish	Goldfish®	-ound	Mounds®
-it	KitKat®	-out	Shout®
-ite	Sprite®, White Rain®	-ow	Dog Chow®
-og	Dog Chow®	-ow	Ivory Snow®, Sweet 'N Low®
-oke	Coke®	-oy	Almond Joy®
-oil	oil	-un	Capri Sun®
-old	Bold®	-ut	Pizza Hut®

Environmental print is popular with young children. Emergent readers enjoy seeing words they know and see everyday in their world. Some young children are surprised to learn that they already know some words and begin to "read" boxes at home and signs as they ride down familiar streets and roads.

Making Names

Making Words (Cunningham and Hall, 1994) is a very popular activity with both teachers and children. Children love manipulating letters to make words and figuring out the secret word which can be made with all the letters. In some of our Making Words lessons, the secret word is a name—perhaps even the name of someone in our classroom or the name of a favorite character from books, movies, or television. Children particularly enjoy making words when the secret word is their name, the name of one of their friends, the teacher's name, or a popular character like **Clifford**, **Garfield**, or **Charlotte**.

While children are having fun making words, they are also learning important information about phonics and spelling. As children manipulate the letters to make the words, they learn how small changes, such as changing just one letter or moving the letters around, result in completely new words. Children learn to stretch out words and listen for the sounds they hear and the order of those sounds. When you change the first letter, you also change the sound you hear at the beginning of the word. Likewise, when you change the last letter, you change the sound you hear at the end of the word. These ideas seem commonplace and obvious to those of us who have been reading and writing for almost as long as we can remember. But they are a revelation to many beginners—and a revelation that gives them tremendous independence in and power over the challenge of decoding and spelling words.

Making Words lessons are an example of a type of instruction called Guided Discovery. In order to truly learn and retain strategies, children must discover them. But some children do not seem to make discoveries about words very easily on their own. In a Making Words lesson, teachers guide students toward those discoveries by carefully sequencing the words they are to make and by giving them explicit guidance about how much change is needed.

Making Words lessons have three steps. The first step is to make words. Teachers begin with short, easy words and move to longer more complex words. The last word is always the secret word—a word that can be made with all of the letters. As children make the words, a child who has it made successfully goes up to the pocket chart or chalk ledge and makes the word with big letters. Children who don't have the word made correctly quickly fix their word to be ready for the next word. The small changes between most words encourages even those children who have not made a word perfectly to fix it because they soon realize that having the current word correctly spelled increases their chances of spelling the next word correctly. In each lesson, children make 9-15 words including the secret word that can be made with all the letters. When it is time to make the secret word, the teacher gives children one minute to try to come up with the word. After one minute, if no one has discovered the secret word, the teacher gives them clues that allow them to figure it out.

The second step of a Making Words Lesson is to sort the words into patterns. Many children discover patterns just through making the words in the carefully sequenced order, but some children need more explicit guidance. This guidance happens when all the words have been made and teachers guide children to sort them into patterns. Depending on the sophistication of the children and the words available in the lesson, words might be sorted according to their beginning letters—all the letters up to the vowel. Alternatively, to focus on just one sound/letter combination, teachers may ask children to sort out all of the words that with qu-, br- or sh-. Once the words with these letters are sorted, the teacher and children pronounce the words and discover that most words that have the same letters also have the same sounds—an important discovery for all emerging readers and writers.

Another pattern which children need to discover is that many words have the same root word. If they can pronounce and spell the root word and if they recognize root words with ending prefixes or suffixes added, they are able to decode and spell many additional words. To some children, every new word they meet is a new experience! They fail to recognize how new words are related to already known words and thus are in the difficult—if not impossible—position of starting from "scratch" and just trying to learn and remember every new word. To be fluent, fast, automatic decoders and spellers, children must learn that **play, playing, played, plays, player,** and **replay** have **play** as their root and use their knowledge of how to decode and spell **play** to quickly transfer to these related words. Whenever possible from the letters available,

Making Words lessons include related words. We tell the children that people are related by blood and words are related by meaning. We ask the children to find any related words and sort them out and then we create sentences to show how these words are related.

In every lesson, the teacher and students sort the rhyming words. Each lesson contains several sets of rhyming words. Children need to recognize that words that have the same spelling pattern from the vowel to the end of the word usually rhyme. When the teacher sorts the words into rhyming words and notices that the words that rhyme have the same spelling pattern, children learn rhyming patterns and how to use words they know to decode and spell lots of other words.

The final step of a Making Words lesson is the transfer step. All of the working and playing with words that is done while making words is worth nothing if children do not use what they know when they need to use it. Many children know letter sounds and patterns and do not apply these to decode an unknown word encountered during reading, or to spell a word they need while writing. All teachers know that it is much easier to teach children phonics than it is to actually get them to use it. This is the reason that every Making Words lesson ends with a transfer step. Once the words are sorted according to rhyme, the teacher tells children to pretend they are reading and come to a new word. As the teacher says this, she writes a word that has the same spelling pattern and rhymes with one set of rhyming words. The teacher shows this word to a child and asks that child to come up and put the new word with the words it rhymes with. The teacher doesn't allow anyone to say the new word until it is lined up under the other rhyming words and then leads the children to pronounce the rhyming words they made and the new word. Then, the teacher shows them one more word and says to a child:

"Pretend you're reading and come to this new word. Put it with the words that would help you figure it out."

Once the teacher has decoded two new words using the rhyming patterns from the words made, she helps the children transfer their letter-sound knowledge to writing. To do this, the teacher asks children to pretend they are writing and need to spell a word:

"Pretend you're writing and you need to spell the word, **stray**. You stretch out **stray** and hear the beginning letters **str-**. If you can think of the words we made today that rhyme with stray you will have the correct spelling of the word."

The children decide that **stray** rhymes with the **-ay** words they made and that **stray** is spelled **s-t-r-a-y**. The teacher finishes the lesson by having students spell one more word by deciding which of the words they made it rhymes with.

A Sample Making Names Lesson

As the person who is teaching the lesson, the teacher is always the best person to decide exactly what to say to children and how to cue them about the different words. If you have a child in your class named Nina, you will cue them differently than a teacher who does not have a Nina. Your students will relate better to example sentences you come up with which relate to their communities and lives. With the caveat that you can do this much better for your children than I—who has never seen your children—here is a sample which you can use to construct your own lesson cues.

Sample Making Names Lesson

The children all have the letters: **a i f k l n n r**. (A Making Words folder for students is available from Carson-Dellosa.) These same letters—big enough for all to see—are displayed in a pocket chart or along the chalk ledge. The vowels are in a different color from the other letters and the letter cards have lower-case letters on one side and capital letters on the other side.

The teacher has written the words the children are going to make on index cards. These will be placed in the pocket chart as the words are made and will be used for the Sort and Transfer steps of the lesson.

Making Names Lesson

Franklin

Make: ink, air, fair, fail, rail, rain, link, rink, rank, Nina, Fran, Frank, final, Franklin

Sort: Fr-words, rhymes

Transfer: thank, think, clink, clank

The teacher begins the lesson by having each child hold up and name each letter as she holds up the big letters in the pocket chart.

"Hold up and name each letter as I hold up the big letter. Let's start with your vowels. Show me your **a** and your **i**. Now show we your **f, k, l,** two **n**'s and **r**. You all have 8 letters. In a few minutes, we will see if anyone can figure out the secret word which uses all 8 letters. Make sure all your letters are showing their lowercase side to start with. When we are making a name, I will cue you and look to see who remembers to turn the first letter in that name to the capital side. Let's get started making words."

Step One: Making Words:

"Use three letters to spell the word **ink**. My pen wouldn't write because it was out of **ink**."

(Find someone with **ink** spelled correctly and send that child to spell **ink** with the big letters.)

"Start over and use 3 letters to spell **air**. The balloon was filled with **air**."

(Quickly send someone with the correct spelling to the big letters. Keep the pace brisk. Do not wait until everyone has air spelled with their little letters. It is fine if some children are making **air** as **air** is being spelled with the big letters.)

"Make sure you have **air** spelled correctly. Add just one letter to spell **fair**. We went to the county **fair**."

(Continue sending children to make the words with the big letters. Remind children to use the big letters to check what they have made with their letters, fixing their own words as needed before going on to the next word. Move the lesson along at a fast pace.)

"Change one letter and you can spell **fail**. I hope I didn't **fail** the test."

"Change just one letter again and you can spell **nail**. I helped my dad **nail** the boards together."

"Change one letter to spell **rail**. The race car crashed into the **rail**."

"Change one letter to spell **rain**. I like to listen to the **rain**."

"Start over and use 4 letters to spell **link**. In math, we use some blocks that **link** together."

"Make sure you have **link** spelled correctly. Change just one letter to spell **rink**. We went to the skating **rink**."

"Change the vowel to spell **rank**. The soldier was promoted to the **rank** of sergeant."

"Start over and use 4 letters to spell the name **Nina**. **Nina** plays the piano."

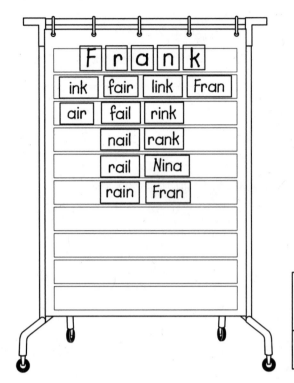

"Start over and use 4 letters to spell the name **Fran**. **Fran** likes to play soccer."

"Add one letter to **Fran** to spell the name **Frank**. My cousin's name is **Frank**."

"Start over and use 5 letters to spell **final**. This is the **final** game of the season."

"I have just one word left. It is the secret word you can make with all your letters. See if you can figure it out."

(Give them one minute to figure out the secret word and then gives clues if needed.)

"Our secret word today is a name that you can spell your letters to a name we already made."

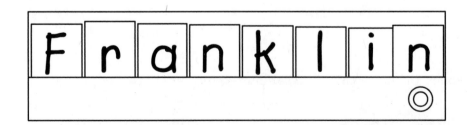

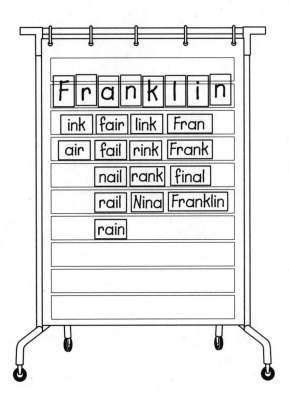

(Let someone go to the big letters and spell the secret word—**Franklin**. Then, let all the children make the word **Franklin** and talk about anyone named **Franklin** that they know. Many children may have read the **Franklin** books.)

Step Two: Sorting the Words into Patterns

Have the children read aloud with you all the words made in the lesson.

Sort Fr Words: (Optional)

If some of your children need review of the fr sound, have them pull out and sort the words that begin with fr. They should pronounce these words, emphasizing the sound of f and r heard at the beginning of all these words.

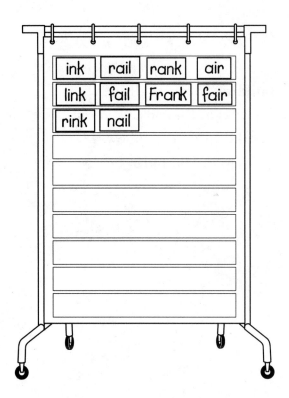

Sort Rhymes:

Send several children to the pocket chart to find rhyming words with the same pattern and line these up with rhymes one under the other.

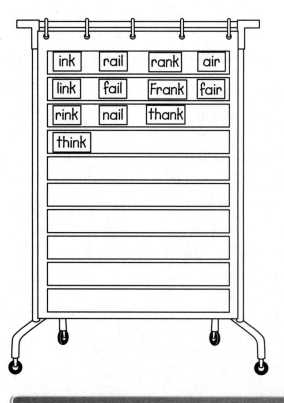

Reading Transfer:

Tell children to pretend they are reading and they come to a new word. Show one child the word **thank** written on an index card. Let that child put **thank** under **rank** and **Frank** and have all of the children pronounce all three words, using the rhyming words they made to decode the new word, **thank**.

Do the same thing with **think**.

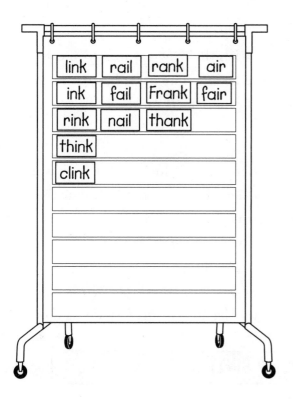

Spelling Transfer:
Tell children to pretend they are writing and need to spell a word.

"Let's pretend Joey is writing and he is trying to spell the word, **clink**."

Have the children tell you that clink begins with **cl-** and write **cl-** on an index card. Then, have children pronounce the sets of rhyming words in the pocket chart and decide that **clink** rhymes with **ink, link,** and **rink** and use the **-ink** pattern to finish spelling **clink**.

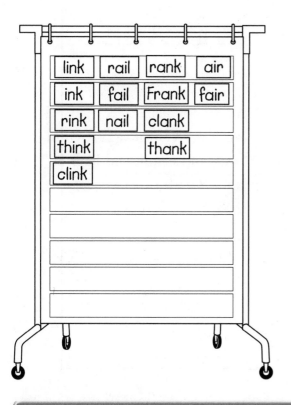

Do the same thing with **clank**.

When you finish the lesson, the rhyming words you made will be lined up in the pocket chart along with two new words they helped you read and two new words they helped you spell.

Making Words Homework

Because students like to manipulate the letters and come up with their own words, you can give them a take-home sheet with the same letters used in the lesson. The sheet has the letters across the top and blocks for writing words. Students write capital letters on the back and then cut apart the letters.

They manipulate the letters to make words and then write them in the blocks. This is a popular homework assignment with students and their parents. When you write the letters at the top, write them in alphabetical order—vowels, then consonants—so as not to give away the secret word. Before children take the sheet home, have them turn it over and write the capital letters on the back. Children love being the "smart" ones who "know the secret word" and watching parents and other relatives try to figure it out. You can use the Making Words Take Home Sheet reproducible on page 137 for making words activities for children to do at home.

Making Names Take-Home Sheet											
a	i	f	k	l	n	n	r				

Making Names is a favorite activity of many children. You can easily plan lessons for the important names in your classroom by going to *www.wordplays.com* and typing in the name. Almost instantly, a list of all the words that can be made with the letters in that name will appear. You can pick and choose the 9-15 words that will make a multilevel lesson with short easy words at the beginning and more complex words at the end. Be sure to include some rhyming words for the Sort and Transfer steps. If there are several words that begin with particular letter combinations you want to emphasize, include them so that you can sort them and notice the letters and sounds. When related words occur, include them and sort for these to help children begin to realize how you decode and spell longer words by recognizing the root word and endings.

It is fun to make your own lessons, but it is also nice to have some "ready to go lessons." Here are ten lessons to get you started. They all use names children might recognize as favorite characters. These lessons were taken from *Making Names* (Cunningham, Carson-Dellosa, 2004) which includes lessons for 210 popular children's names.

Alexander

Make: Ed Ned Rex and land Alan Alex lead/deal real relax leader/dealer relaxed Alexander

Sort: Related Words: lead, leader; deal, dealer; relax, relaxed

Rhymes: and, land deal, real

Transfer: squeal, stand; steal, grand

Barney

Make: ear Ray bay ban ran bran/barn yarn year near earn yearn Barney

Sort: Beginning Letters

Rhymes: Ray, bay; ban, ran, bran; barn, yarn; ear, year, near; earn, yearn

Transfer: learn, clear; stray clan

Casper

Make: ape ace cap car par/rap race pace care scare scrap scrape/Casper

Sort: Scr words: scrap, scrape

Rhymes: ape, scrape; ace, pace, race; car, par; care, scare; rap, scrap, cap

Transfer: space, grape; share scar

Charlotte

Make: heat coat chat Chet Cora Earl each reach teach/cheat treat Carol throat chatter Charlotte

Sort: Related Words: chat, chatter

Rhymes: treat, heat, cheat; coat, throat; each, reach, teach

Transfer: wheat, goat; float, beach

Clifford

Make: of off for old oil coil foil Lori cold fold Ford cord Cliff Clifford

Sort: Beginning Letters

Rhymes: old, cold, fold; Ford, cord; oil coil, foil

Transfer: told, boil; broil, scold

Dorothy

Make: hot rot Rod Roy try dry toy hood hoot root Troy door/odor Dorothy

Sort: Beginning Letters

Rhymes: hot, rot; Roy, Troy; hoot, root; try, dry

Transfer: boot, sky; shoot, shot

Frederick

Make: kid rid Eric Fred Rick Dick fire fired/fried cried/cider rider Derrick Frederick

Sort: Related Words: fire, fired

Rhymes: kid, rid; fried, cried; rider, cider

Transfer: tried, spider; slid, spied

Garfield

Make: die lie age rage Earl lied fail Gail fire fired/fried grade/raged field Garfield

Sort: Related Words: rage, raged; lie, lied; fire, fired

Rhymes: die, lie; age, rage; fail, Gail

Transfer: wage, pail; tie, cage

Madeline

Make: die lie lied mine line Lane mane/name lame Neil named medal Delia Elaine Madeline

Sort: Related Words: name, named; lie, lied

Rhymes: lie, die; mine, line; Lane, mane; name, lame

Transfer: blame, pie; Jane, pine

Rudolph

Make: hop pod Rod old hold drop/prod loud proud holdup/uphold Rudolph

Sort: Beginning Letters

Rhymes: pod, Rod; old, hold; loud, proud; hop, drop

Transfer: cloud, crop; scold, chop

Favorite Read Aloud Books with Names

Chapter 11

Children are never too young or too old to be read to. Reading aloud to children is the single most important factor in developing a child's interest and ability in reading; it creates readers. There are many books to read to children. Some children like a good story; other children like the information found in books. Here are some tips for reading to children.

- Read aloud to your students every day.

- Read aloud something you know and like.

- Choose a variety of materials—a story, a poem, an item in the newspaper or magazine that grabs their interest, a favorite author, a biography, a book about an upcoming holiday, a book about something they are learning about in science or social studies, or a book with a name in the title because you are talking about names.

- Link the story to life or other books.

- Ask the children to predict the outcome.

- Talk about the book (or the name).

- Talk about what you liked (or didn't like) and ask for their opinions.

Picture Books with Names in the Titles

Alexander and the Wind-Up Mouse by Leo Lionni (Bantam Doubleday Dell Books for Young Readers, 1974)

Alexander was lonely until the day he met Willy the wind-up mouse. He envied Willy until it was Annie's birthday and she was discarding Willy for her new toys. Alexander was sad until he gets an idea for his wish with the purple pebble and his wish comes true.

Alexander and the Terrible, Horrible, No Good, Very Bad Day by Judith Viorst (Simon & Schuster Children's, 1976)

Everyone has a bad day once in a while and everyone relates to this story. Alexander starts his day off with the only cereal box without a prize. Sequels by Judith Viorst are: *Alexander, Who Used to Be Rich, Last Sunday* (Scott Foresman, 1987) and *Alexander Who's Not (Do You Hear Me? I Mean It!) Going to Move* (Aladdin Library, 1998).

Amazing Grace by Mary Hoffman (Dial, 1991)

Grace is sad when classmates tell her she can't play Peter Pan because she is a girl and black. After seeing an African-American ballerina perform, Grace knows she can be anything she wants to be.

Amelia Bedelia by Peggy Parrish (HarperCollins, 1983)

Every child's favorite maid is Amelia Bedelia. She means well but takes everything literally and always gets it wrong! Young children laugh as Amelia dusts the furniture by putting powder on it and changes the towels by cutting new designs in them. (There are several other *Amelia Bedelia* books and all are fun to read for a hilarious exploration of homonyms.)

Anansi Goes Fishing by Eric A. Kimmel (Holiday House, Inc., 1997)

Why do spiders spin webs? The reason we learn in this book, is because of the time Anansi, the spider, tried to trick Turtle into catching a fish and cooking it for him. But this time lazy Anasi weaves the nets (webs) and catches the fish while turtle gets to eat the fish. There are several *Anansi the Spider* books and they are all African tales that explain why things happen.

Angelina on Stage by Katharine Holabird (Pleasant Company Publications, 2002)
Angelina's cousin, Henry, liked to go to her ballet lessons at Miss Lilly's house and join in the dancing. Then, Miss Lilly receives a letter and asks Angelina to be a magic fairy in a real grown-ups' ballet; Henry would have a small part in the play. At rehearsals, Angelina learned to fly through the air on a wire attached to her costume. After finding and helping Henry one day, she too gets a speaking part.

Annie and the Old One by Miska Miles (Little, Brown & Co., 1985)
This is the story of a loving relationship between a Native American girl and her grandmother. The story is about Annie who does not want her grandmother to get old. She tries to prevent her grandmother from finishing a rug because her grandmother has said that when she completes the rug she is weaving, she will go to Mother Earth. When Annie accepts the inevitable, she picks up the weaving stick and helps her grandmother complete the rug.

Anno's Alphabet by Mitsumasa Anno (HarperCollins Children's Books, 1975)
An alphabet book written especially for young children. They love to search the pictures to find and name the objects beginning with the same letter. Other *Anno* books by Mitsumasa Anno include: *Anno's Counting Book* (HarperTrophy, 1986), *Anno's Journey* (Puffin, 1997).

Arthur's Family Vacation by Marc Brown (Little, Brown and Co., 1995)
Arthur's family plans and goes on a vacation to the seashore. This aardvark family's vacation, like many human families, looks like a disaster because it rains and the motel room is too small. Arthur decides to plan field trips to amuse the family until the last day when the sun shines and the family spends a glorious day at the beach. There are many other *Arthur* books in this popular series where this aardvark family looks, dresses, and acts like humans.

Babar's Family Album: Five Favorite Stories by Laurent De Brunhoff (Random House, Incorporated 1991)
An old favorite; five stories of Babar the elephant and his family are published in one volume.

My Brown Bear Barney by Dorothy Butler (HarperCollins Children's Books, 2001)
The story of a little girl who likes to take her brown bear Barney everywhere she goes; until she goes to school and mother says she can't take Barney with her!

Bedtime for Frances by Russell Hoban (HarperTrophy, 1976)
Frances the badger cannot get to sleep. All the ploys of the little children to avoid bedtime, all the fears of nighttime, are treated with gentle humor here. Other *Frances* books by Russell Hoban include: *A Baby Sister for Frances* (HarperTrophy, 1976); *Best Friends for Frances* (HarperTrophy, 1976); *A Birthday for Frances* (HarperTrophy, 1976); *Bread and Jam for Frances* (HarperTrophy, 1993).

Chrysanthemum by Kevin Henkes (Morrow, William & Co, 1996)
This is a story about a name that has become very popular lately. Chrysanthemum loves her name. She thinks it's perfect until she starts going to school and the other children make fun of it. Now she is not sure if Chrysanthemum is the perfect name anymore. A kind teacher helps Chrysanthemum solve this problem.

Clifford the Big Red Dog by Norman Bridwell (Scholastic, Inc., 1985)
Clifford the big red dog is a favorite of many young children. This is the first in a series of books written about America's biggest, reddest, and most-loved dog.

Corduroy by Don Freeman (Puffin, 1976)
This is a story about a teddy bear's search through a department store for a friend. His quest ends when a girl buys him with savings from her piggybank. Other *Corduroy* books by Don Freeman include: *A Pocket for Corduroy* (Puffin, 1989); *Corduroy's Christmas Surprise* (Grosset and Dunlap, 2000).

Curious George by H.A. Rey (Houghton Mifflin Company, 1973)
This is one of the old favorites in children's books. George is a funny little monkey who was found in Africa and brought to this country on a ship by the "man in the yellow hat." George's curiosity gets him in trouble time after time. There are many other Curious George books in this series.

Danny and the Dinosaur by Syd Hoff (HarperCollins Children's Books, 1978)
An "I Can Read Book" that's a favorite when young children ask for a dinosaur story. Danny visits a museum where a friendly dinosaur offers to go home and play with Danny and his friends.

David Goes to School by David Shannon (Scholastic, Inc., 1999)
The author uses cartoon art to create a portrait of a perfectly believable, but impossible, little boy. *No, David!* (Scholastic, 1998) is another book by David Shannon, who often heard the word "no" when he was a child.

Dustin's Big School Day by Alden R. Carter (Albert Whitman, 1999)
Dustin is a Down's syndrome child in a regular second-grade class. This is the story of an important-to-Dustin school day. The day when friends of his father, Dave and Skippy (a puppet), are coming to school to put on a show for the students. We get to see the whole day in school, what Dustin does, and who teaches him what as he awaits this special event. *Big Brother Dustin* (Alden Carter, Albert Whitman and Company, 1997) is the first book in the series.

Doctor DeSoto Goes to Africa by William Steig (HarperCollins, 1994)
If you liked the first book—*Doctor DeSoto* (William Steig, Sunburst, 1990)—then you will like this one, too. The good mouse dentist hurries off to Africa when an elephant complains of a toothache and is kidnapped, setting off a chain of impossible events.

Elizabeti's Doll by Stephanie Stuve-Bodeen (Lee and Low Books, 2000)
Elizabeti's mother has a new baby to take care of. His name is Obedia. Elizabeti pretends a rock is her doll and names it Eva. She imitates her mother's loving care of the new baby.

In the sequel, *Mama Elizabeti* (Stephanie Stuve-Bodeen, Lee and Low Books, 2000), her mother has another new baby and Elizabeti must take care of Obedia. She finds he is not as easy to care for as her rock was!

Franklin series by Pauline Bourgeois (Scholastic, Inc.)
There are many books by Pauline Bourgeois in this series: *Franklin Goes to School* (Scholastic, Inc., 1995), *Franklin Rides a Bike* (Scholastic, Inc., 1997), *Franklin in the Dark* (Scholastic, Inc., 1987), *Franklin's New Friend* (Scholastic, Inc., 1997), etc. Each book is about a problem and how Franklin solves his problem.

Frederick by Leo Lionni (Dragonfly, 1967)
Frederick is a tiny, gray field mouse. While his brothers and sisters gather food for the oncoming winter, Frederick gathers the colors and stories and dreams they will need to sustain them through the cold winter darkness. It turns out that Frederick is a poet and knows it!

Hattie and the Fox by Mem Fox (Bradbury, 1988)
The story of a hen and some farm animals, with lots of repetitive print. When Hattie, a black barnyard hen, sees something in the woods none of the other animals seems to care. When the "something" turns out to be a fox, the other animals are surprised.

Henry and Mudge by Cynthia Rylant (Bradbury, 1991)
Henry worries whether his grandmother will like his beloved dog, Mudge. Will Mudge drool on Grandma? Will Mudge have to sleep outside? These are some things Henry worries about as he is going all alone, on a trip to Grandma's house. The *Henry and Mudge* books that follow in this series are delightful beginning readers about the adventures of Henry and his dog, Mudge.

Ira Sleeps Over by Bernard Weber (Houghton Mifflin Co., 1973)
This is a story about a boy who spends the night at his friend's house. The story centers around the boy's struggle over whether or not to bring a teddy bear along. It makes for a lively discussion about individual sleeping habits, peer pressure, and things we hold on to.

Johnny Appleseed retold by Steven Kellogg (Scholastic, Inc., 1988)
This is the story of Johnny Appleseed, a great American frontier hero who planted apple trees as he set out across the country. Johnny Chapman's (his real name) retellings of his adventures inspired others to tell tales about him and life on the American frontier.

John Henry by Julius Lester (Dial Books, 1994)
John Henry is an African-American folk hero. John Henry was strong and grew up fast. Soon he was bursting through the porch roof, breaking boulders for roads, and helping dig through a mountain. Nothing could stop John Henry! But, John Henry's heart burst after hammering so hard and so fast through the mountain one day. They say he was buried late one night on the lawn of the White House in Washington, D.C. while the president slept.

Leo the Late Bloomer by Robert Kraus (Windmill, 1971)
Leo, a young tiger, cannot read, write, talk, draw, or even eat neatly. Leo's father keeps watching for signs of big tiger behavior from little Leo. His mother suggests he is just a late bloomer. Leo does bloom, and in his own good time he can do everything he couldn't do before.

Lilly's Purple Plastic Purse by Kevin Henkes (Greenwillow, 1996)
Lilly really likes her teacher, Mr. Slinger. One day, she takes her purple plastic purse, shiny coins, and sunglasses to school, because she wants to show them off. Mr. Slinger, however, takes them away from her and she writes a mean note to the teacher she no longer likes.

Madeline by Ludwig Bemelmans (Viking, 1958)
The classic story of Madeline and her schoolmates, "twelve little girls in two straight lines," who live in an old house in Paris. Madeline is a constant challenge to Miss Clavel. The author's use of rhyming verse, daring adventure, and naughtiness make it a favorite for young children year after year.

There are four other books by Ludwig Bemelmans in this series: *Madeline and the Bad Hat* (Viking Press, 1957), *Madeline and the Gypsies* (Viking Press, 1959), *Madeline in London* (Viking Press, 1961), and *Madeline's Rescue* (Viking Press, 1953).

Mirandy and Brother Wind by Patricia McKissack (Knopf, 1988)
Mirandy schemes to get Brother Wind to help her win the Junior Cakewalk dance contest in her rural South during the 1920s.

Speak English for Us, Marisol! by Karen English (Albert Whitman Co., 2000)
Marisol, who is bilingual, is sometimes overwhelmed when her Spanish-speaking family members and neighbors need her to translate for them. This is a familiar story in many American classrooms today as students help parents to understand what is happening at their school.

Miss Bindergarten Stays Home from Kindergarten by Joseph Slate (Dutton Books, 2000)
Another book about Miss Bindergarten written in rhyme. It is the story of what happens the day Miss Bindergarten does not show up for school and the children have their first "substitute." Other *Miss Bindergarten* books by Joseph Slate include: *Miss Bindergarten Takes a Field Trip with Kindergarten* (Dutton Books, 2001); *Miss Bindergarten Celebrates the 100th Day of Kindergarten* (Puffin, 2002).

Miss Nelson Is Missing by Harry Allard (Scholastic, 1978)
Miss Nelson is kind and beautiful but cannot control her class. When she is suddenly absent, the children begin to realize what a wonderful teacher they had in Miss Nelson. Her substi-

tute is the strict Viola Swamp, who works the class incessantly. The class wants Miss Nelson back. When will she return? Another *Miss Nelson* book by Harry Allard is *Miss Nelson Is Back* (Houghton Mifflin, Co., 1986).

Miss Rumphius by Barbara Cooney (Penguin, 1982)
Grandfather tells young Alice she must make the world more beautiful when she grows up. And that is just what she does, planting seeds all over the countryside.

Mortimer by Robert Munch (Annick Press Ltd., 1985)
One night, Mortimer's mother put him to bed and told him to be quiet. He wasn't! Up came father, seventeen brothers and sisters, then the policemen; but Mortimer wouldn't be quiet. Mortimer finally fell asleep waiting for someone else to come up.

Mufaro's Beautiful Daughters by John Steptoe (HarperTrophy, 1993)
A Cinderella story set in Africa. In this story, one sister is kind and caring, and one is vain. They compete for the king's hand in marriage.

My Great Aunt Arizona by Gloria Houston (HarperCollins, 1992)
Arizona was born in a big cabin her papa built. She grew into a tall girl who liked to sing, square dance, and most of all read and dream of far away places she would visit one day. Instead, she became a teacher in a one-room school house where she touched many lives.

Nettie's Trip South by Ann Turner (Aladdin Paperbacks, 1995)
A story inspired by great-grandmother Henrietta's diary of her trip south in 1859 when she was ten years old. She travels on her first train trip with her brother and sister hoping to see the south before the war breaks out and travel may not be safe. She sees slaves, a slave auction, and the sights and sounds of a southern city, then returns home an abolitionist.

Olivia by Ian Falconer (Scholastic, Inc., 2000)
Olivia is a wonderful pig who believes she can do anything she wants to do. She sees herself as a ballerina, a builder of great buildings, and even an artist. When she paints a wall at home, she gets in trouble and earns a "time out." Other *Olivia* books by Ian Falconer are available.

Peter's Chair by Ezra Jack Keats (HarperCollins, 1967)
Peter is upset and runs away when he sees his crib, cradle, and high chair painted pink for the new baby until he realizes how important it is to be a big brother.

Rachel Parker, Kindergarten Show Off by Ann Martin (Scholastic, Inc., 1993)
Olivia loves kindergarten. She is smart; she can read and write. Then, Rachel Parker moves next door, she's smart too. Olivia thinks Rachel Parker is the world's biggest show off!

The Story of Ruby Bridges by Robert Coles (Scholastic, Inc., 1995)
Ruby Bridges was born in Mississippi and was someone who changed the United States and became part of history. Ruby was the first black child to go to an all-white (segregated) school in Mississippi. White parents did not send their children to school and Ruby was there alone with her teacher Miss Hurley. Each day Ruby says a prayer before and after school to forgive the angry people outside of the school.

Sarah Morton's Day by Kate Waters (Scholastic, Inc., 1989)
Sarah Morton is a Pilgrim girl who lived in Plymouth colony long ago. Sarah's day begins at sun-up with tending the fire and feeding the chickens. There is time for playing with her friend Elizabeth and for a brief reading lesson during her busy day. How does Sarah's day compare to children's days today?

Some of the Days of Everett Anderson by Lucille Clifton (Henry Holt and Co., 1987)
This is the story of an African-American boy and his family. Strong family ties are found in this book and all of the *Everett Anderson* books by Lucille Clifton that follow—*Everett Anderson's Friend* (Henry Holt and Co., 1992), *Everett Anderson's Nine Months Long* (Henry Holt and Co., 1978), *Everett Anderson's Year* (Henry Holt and Co., 1992), *Everett Anderson's Goodbye* (Henry Holt and Co., 1983), and *Everett Anderson's Christmas Coming* (Henry Holt and Co., 1991).

Stellaluna by Janell Cannon (Scholastic, Inc., 1993)
Stellaluna is a baby bat. An owl attacks her mother and she is dropped. Luckily, she becomes caught in a tree, and is raised by some birds. Soon, Stellaluna loses her bat ways and eats bugs and sleeps in the nest at night like the bird family. One day, she meets a bat who is really her mother and she finds out she is not a bird but a bat!

Stevie by John Steptoe (HarperCollins, 1969)
The art in this picture book helps emphasize the alienation between Robert, the narrator of this story, and the child his mother baby-sits, Stevie. The boys later become friends.

Strega Nona by Tomie dePaola (Prentice Hall, 1975)
Strega Nona could do magic and cure headaches and other problems. Big Anthony tries to discover the secrets of Strega Nona's magic and has to eat the consequences of his own foolishness.

Sweet Clara and the Freedom Quilt by Deborah Hopkinson (Alfred Knopf, 1993)
Clara was a young girl sent from North Farm to Home Plantation to work in the fields. There she learned to sew from Aunt Rachel and began working in the big house instead of the fields. She learns about run away slaves, the Underground Railroad and freedom in the North and Canada. Piecing together scrapes of cloth and information from those who visit the big house she begins her map to freedom, a quilt.

Sylvester and the Magic Pebble by William Steig (Simon & Schuster, 1969)
This picture book won the Caldecott Medal in 1969 for the best picture book that year. Young Sylvester finds a magic pebble that will grant his every wish as long as he holds it in his hand. When a hungry lion approaches, Sylvester wishes himself into a stone. Since stones don't have hands, the pebble drops to the ground and Sylvester cannot pick it up to wish himself normal again. Both Sylvester and his parents are sad until they are happily reunited a year later.

The Tale of Peter Rabbit by Beatrix Potter (Scholastic, Inc., 1987)
This is one of the most famous animal stories of all times. The tale of a naughty rabbit full of adventure, he goes where he has been told not to go, to Mr. McGregor's garden. He narrowly escapes and returns home. His mother finds out and he suffers the consequences. Other books by Beatrix Potter include: *The Tale of Benjamin Bunny* (Penguin Books, Ltd., 1993) and *The Tale of Tom Kitten* (Dover, 1995).

When Sophie Gets Angry—Really, Really Angry by Molly Bang (Scholastic, Inc., 1999)
In this story, Sophie's anger is graphically depicted with color. The madder she gets the redder the color. When Sophie actually has a screaming fit, she looks like she may actually explode

and runs off to the woods. There her anger gradually subsides and she returns home her old self with a sunny disposition.

Wilfrid Gordon MacDonald Patridge by Mem Fox (Kane/Miller Book Publishers, 1985)
A small boy tries to find the meaning of "memory" so he can help Miss Nancy, who lives next door at the old people's home, find hers. He does it with a basket of wonderful things that has Miss Nancy remembering her past treasures.

William's Doll by Charlotte Zolotow (Harper, 1972)
William's father wants him to play with his baseball or trains, William, to the surprise of all wishes he had a doll to play with. When everyone thinks he's a sissy his grandmother says something else. An important message for young boys (and maybe their fathers, brothers, and others family members!)

Yeh Shen: A Cinderella Story from China retold by Ai-Ling Louie (Philomel, 1990)
A Cinderella version from China. Children like to compare this version with the one they know or have read and talk about the differences in the Cinderella stories: the stepmother, the sisters, what happens when she meets the prince.

Yolanda's Genius by Carol Fenner (Simon and Schuster, 1995)
Yolanda's positive attitude creates strong characterization in this story about sister and brother relationships.

Zomo the Rabbit: A Trickster Tale from West Africa by Gerald McDermott (Voyager Books, 1996)
This is a story about a rabbit who uses wit, trickery, and courage but lacks caution. The moral of the tale is that the three things worth having are: courage, good sense, and caution.

Familiar Folktales with Names in the Titles
(There are many versions of these tales and can be found in single volumes or anthologies.)

Cinderella
This story is found around the world in many versions and has been retold in many languages. It is the story of a sweet girl and two cruel sisters and how she meets and marries the prince.

Goldilocks and the Three Bears

Another favorite story retold by many. This is the story of a little girl who goes into the woods by herself and enters the home of the three bears. She sits in their chair, eats the food, and then climbs into their beds. What a surprise when the bears come home and find Goldilocks sleeping there!

Hansel and Gretel

This is the story of a wicked stepmother, weak father, and two smart children.

Henny Penny

This is the story of a hen who thinks that the sky is falling and runs around town warning everyone.

Jack and the Beanstalk

This is the story of a boy named Jack who climbs a beanstalk (tree) and encounters a giant. There are many wonderful versions of this retold tale.

Little Red Hen

Poor Little Red Hen! She finds a grain of wheat then ends up doing all of the work. First, she plants the wheat. Then, she cares for the plants, harvests them, and grinds the wheat into flour. Who will help? No one! When she makes the bread, she finds she has friends. Who wants to eat it? They do!

Little Red Riding Hood

The popular story of a little girl who goes to visit her grandmother. When she gets there, the wolf is in her grandmother's bed. "What big eyes you have!" "What big ears you have!" "What a big mouth!" Red Riding Hood finds that it is not her grandmother but a wolf. Luckily she is rescued by a woodcutter passing by.

Rapunzel

This is the story of a beautiful girl, named Rapunzel, who is held captive high up in a castle. The prince calls, "Rapunzel, Rapunzel, let down your long hair!" She lets her hair down, and up he climbs so he can see her. What happens when they are found?

Rumpelstiltskin
This is the story of a little man (dwarf) who, for a fee, helps a little girl spin straw into gold. In the best-known Grimm's version, the man demands her first-born child as payment.

Snow White and the Seven Dwarfs
Snow White lives with seven dwarfs until she meets the handsome prince and lives happily ever after.

The Three Billy Goats Gruff
There are three goats named Gruff and they want to cross over a bridge. Under the bridge lives a troll. As each goat crosses over the bridge, he promises the troll a better meal is coming next. They all trick the troll and make it across the bridge to the greener grass on the other side.

Easy Chapter Books

Cam Jansen and the Mystery of the Dinosaur Bones by David Adler (Viking Press, 1981)
Cam Jansen is a school-age detective. Follow the clues and try to figure out this and other easy-to-read *Cam Jansen* mysteries.

Charlotte's Web by E. B. White (Harper, 1952)
One of the most universally acclaimed books by children and adults and one of the most read in schools. The story centers on the barnyard life of a young pig who is slated to be butchered in the fall. The animals of the yard (particularly a haughty spider named Charlotte) conspire with the farmer's daughter to save the pig. A wonderful story of friendship and life cycles.

Encyclopedia Brown Takes the Cake by Donald Sobol (Scholastic, Inc., 1991)
This easy-to-read mystery is about a boy called Encyclopedia Brown. Children can follow the clues and try to solve the case. There are several books in this popular series by Donald Sobol.

Flat Stanley by Jeff Brown (Harper Collins, 1964)
Stanley Lambchop is awakened one morning to discover that he has been squashed flat by a falling bulletin board during the night. One of the many advantages is that Flat Stanley can now visit friends traveling in an envelope and sent through the mail. A funny and easy-to-read chapter book. There is a sequel, *Stanley, Flat Again!* by Jeff Brown (HarperTrophy, 2004).

Julian's Glorious Summer by Ann Cameron (Random House, 1987)
Julian starts some major trouble when he can't admit to his friend Gloria that he is afraid to ride a bike. Other Julian titles by Ann Cameron are: *Stories Julian Tells* (Yearling Books, 1989) and *More Stories Julian Tells* (Yearling, 1989).

Junie B. Jones Series by Barbara Park (Random House)
This series begins with a kindergarten student who "tells it like it is." Each easy-to-read chapter book keeps listeners and readers laughing. Recently, Junie B. Jones went to first grade—at last!

Ramona the Pest by Beverly Cleary (HarperTrophy, 1992)
This is a book about Ramona in her early months of kindergarten. We learn about her first day of school, show and tell, seat work, and a substitute teacher. (Other books in the series by Beverly Cleary include: *Ramona and Her Father* (HarperTrophy, 1999); *Ramona and Her Mother* (HarperTrophy, 1990); *Ramona Quimby, Age 8* (HarperTrophy, 1992); and *Ramona the Brave* (HarperTrophy, 1995).

Sarah Plain and Tall by Patricia MacLachlan (HarperCollins, 1985)
When Papa advertises for a new wife, Anna and Caleb try to recall memories of their mother. Sarah comes to live with them on the prairie and soon the children love Sarah.

Most biographies are books with names in the titles and have not been included on this list but are a vast source of names books.

Reading to children creates readers. Choose picture books and some easy chapter books for variety. Include fiction and informational books in your choices. Introduce students to the wonderful world of children's literature with old favorites and new books. Many of the characters like George or Madeline will be friends long after the reading is finished.

Teaching Math
with Names

Chapter 12

You can use your children's names to teach math. Children pay better attention when they can relate mathematical concepts to their own names. Even when the name being used is someone else's name, children compare that name with their name and predict the answer for their own names. You will hear children saying things like:

"My name has even more letters."

"I can add my name to Jim and get 7 letters too."

When you hear these responses, you know the children are actively thinking about the mathematical concepts and relating them to themselves. There are many math activities you can do using the names. Here are some to get you started. Once you start using the names, you will think of lots more.

Counting

To prepare for this activity, make name necklaces for all of your students. Print each first name clearly on a large index card or sentence strip with a black permanent marker, or print the names on a computer using a large, clear font. Underline each letter in each name. Laminate and punch two holes in each card. Attach yarn so that the names can be worn like necklaces.

The simplest counting activity is to have all of the children count the letters in each child's name. Choose a child to point to the letters as everyone counts.

You can move to higher numbers by calling three or four children to the front and having everyone count all the letters in these names. You might want children to make a guess (estimate) before they count and see how close their guesses come.

How many letters do all of the boys' first names have? Get all of the boys up front and find out. How many letters do all of the girls' names have? If the children are seated by tables, count the letters in the names of the children at each table. Count all of the letters in everyone's name and get the grand total!

You can combine letter name instruction with counting. Have all of the children whose names contain the letter **a** come forward and have the children count the **a**'s. Do the same with **b**'s, **c**'s, etc. Be sure to include a letter which no one has in their names if you have one. The counting answer to this question is zero!

Odd or Even Numbers

After counting the letters in all of the names, have children go to one side of the room if their names have an odd number of letters and to the other side of the room if their names have an even number. You may want to have children count the letters in their first and last names and decide if they are an odd/odd (both names have an odd number of letters), even/even, odd/even, or even/odd.

Graphing

Do some of the counting activities again but this time, graph the answers. You may want to graph the number of letters in each child's name.

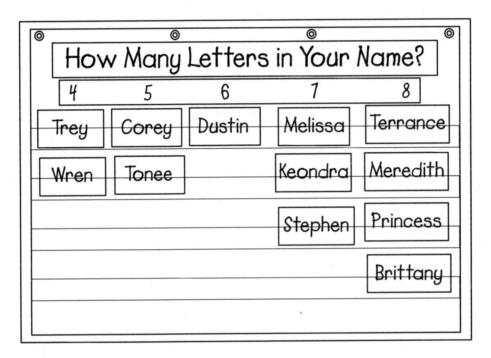

You can also graph the names together by how many letters they have.

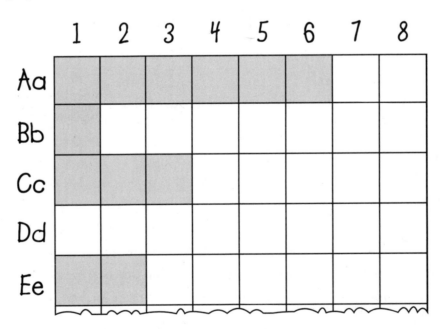

If you counted to see how many of each letter of the alphabet you have, you can graph this, too.

For older children, you may want to teach them how to plot their names on a graph. Let the vertical axis be the number of letters in their first names and the horizontal axis be the number of letters in their last names. Have each child count up the number of letters in her first name and the number of letters in her last name. Write each name where it goes.

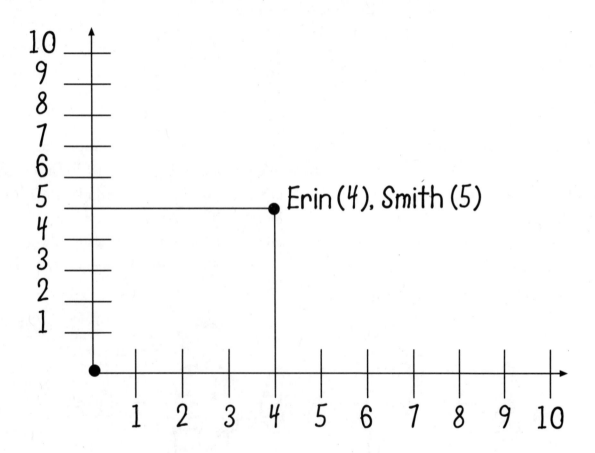

Greater than (>), Less than (<), or Equal to (=)
Print and laminate cards for the greater than (>), less than (<), and equal (=) signs. Have all of the children put on their name necklaces and call up pairs of children to stand next to one another. Have the other children decide which sign should be put between the names and have a child hold that sign there.

Another activity children like is to have one child come up with his name and pick one of the sign cards. Next, all of the children in the class who could make the greater than (or less than or equal to) sentence true come and stand on the other side of the sign. If you let the chosen child hold up the other two signs, every child in the class will have a chance to come up and complete the math sentence. The children will discover that the number of letters in the chosen child's name will be greater than, less than, or equal to all of the other names in the class.

If you made graphs of the number of letters in the names, have the children compare the graphs and use the correct greater than, less than, or equal to terms and signs.

Addition

Children love doing name addition. The simplest form of name addition has children adding up the letters in various names.

How much is Al + Barbara?

Barbara + Cassandra?

Al + Cassandra?

You can also do three- and four-digit addition by including three or four names in each column. Children fill in the numbers and add, counting the letters if they need to check.

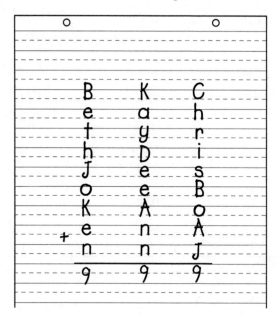

You can also pose more sophisticated addition questions:

"Which two names when added together will give you the largest number?"

"Which two names when added together will give you the smallest number?"

"Which other names can be combined to give you the same number of letters as Al + Barbara?"

Children can add the letters in their first and last names and see what totals they come up with. A more sophisticated addition activity using the names is to do "What's Your Name Number." Display a chart assigning points to each letter.

What's Your Name Number?		
Allie = 39	Aa-1	Pp-16
Taylor = 91	Bb-2	Qq-17
Jessica = 66	Cc-3	Rr-18
Ashley = 70	Dd-4	Ss-19
Sarah = 47	Ee-5	Tt-20
Rachel = 47	Ff-6	Uu-21
Angelica = 52	Gg-7	Vv-22
Tracy = 67	Hh-8	Ww-23
Lenzi = 66	Ii-9	Xx-24
Neha = 28	Jj-10	Yy-25
	Kk-11	Zz-26
	Ll-12	
	Mm-13	
	Nn-14	
	Oo-15	

Each child writes the letters in his name (or a classmate's name) going down. Then, he puts the number of points next to each letter and adds the numbers. Who has the most? The least?

J (10) + **a** (1) + **y** (25) + **l** (12) + **e** (5) + **n** (14) = 67

P (16) + **a** (1) + **t** (20) = 37

Include last names and you will get some big totals. Have children predict whether their first or last names have the largest total.

Another variation of this is to do name scrabble. Just as in regular Scrabble®, common letters get fewer points and less common letters get more points.

Subtraction

Subtraction activities are similar to addition activities but you have to start with the name with the larger number of letters.

How much is Christopher – Juan? Juan – Jim?

What other names can you subtract and get the same answer as Christopher – Juan?

What names can you use and get the answer of zero?

What name can you subtract from Patricia to get Jim?

Problem Solving

Problem solving uses all of the operations discussed previously, but children have to decide what operation to do. Make up some problems and then let children make up some for each other to solve.

Which first (last) name has the greatest number of letters?

Which first (last) name has the least number of letters?

Which first (last) names have an equal number of letters?

How many names have more than six (four, five) letters?

How many names have less than six (seven, eight) letters?

How many total letters do Pablo and Hannah have in their first and last names?

How many names begin with m? End with m? Have an m in them? Have more than one m?

Which first (last) names have a name number greater than 60?

Which names have exactly twice as many letters as Pat? Three times as many letters?

Whose name equals the number of letters in Charlie minus the number of letters in Carl?

Make up two different names whose name numbers would be more than 50 (61, 73).

Whose name has the most (least) Scrabble® points?

Make up a name worth exactly 20 (26, 32) Scrabble® points.

Choose five names of friends or relatives or pets and bar graph their names.

Choose five names of friends or relatives or pets and plot graph their first and last names.

Children's names are not only ideal for teaching reading and writing but are also ideal for teaching math. Children will be more interested in counting, graphing, adding, subtracting, comparing numbers, and problem solving when their names are a major focus in these activities. The activities in this chapter are just a few of the many possibilities for using names to teach math.

Assessing Phonics Skills with Names

Chapter 13

Assessing what children know about letters and sounds is easier said than done. It is easy enough to say a word with a particular sound and have children tell you what letter makes that sound, or to show a letter and ask children to make that sound. This, however, will not tell you very much about what children can actually do with their letter-sound knowledge. Many children can tell you the sounds of letters but cannot figure out unknown words with those letter combinations. To really know what phonics skills children have, you need to ask them to read new words containing the targeted sounds.

This, too, is easier said than done. Once children are reading, they recognize many words they have read before without having to decode those words. Imagine that you want to know if a child can decode words with the common sound for the vowel **a**. If you have the child pronounce common words such as **clay, back,** and **star** to determine their ability to decode words with the vowel **a** and they correctly pronounce them, you don't know if they decoded those words or if those were sight words learned from their previous reading. For this reason, some tests use nonsense words to test decoding skills. The child might be asked to pronounce made-up words such as **glay, dack,** and **smar.** Nonsense words solve the problem of the child's knowing the words as sight words but nonsense words have another problem. Good readers ask themselves questions such as "Did that make sense?" and "Did that sound right?" Asking these questions is a very important reading strategy because it allows students to self-correct errors made and to constantly check their decoding with the context of what they are read- ing. Reading nonsense words violates this self-checking strategy good readers use and many good readers will mispronounce the nonsense words by making them into real words they have heard of. Glay might be pronounced as **"gray"** or **"glad."** Dack might be **"back"** or **"deck."** Smar might be pronounced **"smart."** Because children tend to want to make nonsense words into "words they have heard of," tests that use nonsense words often result in children showing less phonics ability than they actually have.

There is one type of word, however, which children hear often—and thus have in their listening vocabularies—but which they don't read often—and thus are not apt to have already learned as sight words. Names are heard all over the place. Names are a big part of every TV and radio program, and usually these names are pronounced but not read. Names are one type of word that most children have more of in their listening vocabularies than in their sight vocabularies; thus, names can be the source of words to measure decoding ability not confounded by context.

In addition to their more-often-heard-than-read quality, names have another advantage for a word-reading test. People do sometimes read lists of names. Teachers and others often "call the role," thus reading a list is a somewhat more natural real-reading task than most other word-list reading tasks. The Names Test (Cunningham, 1990; Duffelmeyer et al., 1999) was developed to help teachers reliably assess decoding ability using a real-life reading task.

You can read more about the initial "Names Test" in "The Names Test: A Quick Assessment of Decoding Ability" (Cunningham, 1990). Read more about the enhanced test in "Further Validation and Enhancement of the Names Test" (Duffelmeyer et al., 1999).

Administering the Names Test

Copy the reproducible list on page 140 or print the names on index cards. Make another list on which you can record responses or copy the response sheets on pages 141 and 142.

Ask a child to pretend that she is a teacher and this is the list of names of the students in the class. Have the child read the list, as if she is taking attendance.

Use a check to indicate correct responses and write the phonetic spelling for any incorrect responses given by the child. If the child does not attempt a name, write "no" next to that name and encourage the child to continue. For polysyllabic words, consider the word correct regardless of where the child places the accent on the word.

Analyze the child's responses, looking for patterns indicative of decoding strengths and weaknesses.

Keep a record of each child's responses and give the test again after several weeks or months of instruction as an indicator of growth in the ability to decode words.

References and Reproducibles

Professional References

Clay, M. (1985) *The Early Detection of Reading Difficulties. Third Edition*. Portsmouth, NH: Heinemann.

Cunningham, P. M. (2004) *Making Names*. Greensboro, NC: Carson-Dellosa Publishing Co.

Cunningham, P. M. "Beginning Reading without Readiness: Structural Language Experience." *Reading Horizons*. (Spring 1979): 222-227.

Cunningham, P. M. and Hall, D. P. (1994) *Making Words*. Carthage, IL: Good Apple.

Duffelmeyer, F. A. et al. "Further Validation and Enhancement of the Names Test." In *Reading Assessment: Principles and Practices for Elementary Teachers: A Collection of Articles from The Reading Teacher*, edited by Shelby J. Barrentine. Newark, DE: International Reading Association, 1999.

Ericson, L. and Juliebo, M. (1998) *The Phonological Awareness Handbook for Kindergarten and Primary Teachers*. Newark, DE: International Reading Association.

Fitzpatrick, J. (1997) *Phonemic Awareness: Playing with Sounds to Strengthen Beginning Reading Skills*. Cypress, CA: Creative Teaching Press.

Hajdusiewicz, B. B. (1998) *Phonics through Poetry: Teaching Phonemic Awareness Using Poetry*. Glenview, IL: Goodyear.

Hall, D. P. (2001) *Making Alphabet Books to Teach Letters and Sounds*. Greensboro, NC: Carson-Dellosa Publishing Co.

Hall, D. P. and Cunningham, P. M. (1997, 2003) *Month-by-Month Reading, Writing, and Phonics for Kindergarten*. Greensboro, NC: Carson-Dellosa Publishing Co.

Hall, D. P. and Loman, K. L. (2002) *Interactive Charts*. Greensboro, NC: Carson-Dellosa Publishing Co.

Hall, D. P. and Williams, E. (2001) *Predictable Charts*. Greensboro, NC: Carson-Dellosa Publishing Co.

Stauffer, R. G. (1970) *The Language-Experience Approach to the Teaching of Reading*. New York: Harper Row.

Van Allen, R. V. and Allen, C. (1966) *Language Experiences in Reading: Teachers' Resource Book*. Chicago, IL: Encyclopedia Brittanica Press.

Children's Books

ABCD: An Alphabet Book of Cats and Dogs by Sheila Moxley (Little, Brown & Company, 2001)

Alexander and the Terrible, Horrible, No Good, Very Bad Day by Judith Viorst (Simon & Schuster Children's, 1976)

Alexander and the Wind-Up Mouse by Leo Lionni (Bantam Doubleday Dell Books for Young Readers, 1974)

Alexander Who's Not (Do You Hear Me? I Mean It!) Going to Move by Judith Viorst (Aladdin Library, 1998)

Alexander, Who Used to Be Rich, Last Sunday by Judith Viorst (Scott Foresman, 1987)

All about Arthur (An Absolutely Absurd Ape) by Eric Carle (Franklin Watts, Inc., 1974)

Alphabet Annie Announces an All-American Album by Marcia O'Shell and Susan Purviance (Houghton Mifflin Company, 1988)

Amazing Grace by Mary Hoffman (Dial, 1991)

Amelia Bedelia by Peggy Parrish (HarperCollins, 1983)

A, My Name is Alice by Jane Bayer (Puffin, 1992)

Anansi Goes Fishing by Eric A. Kimmel (Holiday House, Inc., 1997)

Angelina on Stage by Katharine Holabird (Pleasant Company Publications, 2002)

Animalia by Graeme Base (Harry N. Abrams, 1987)

Annie and the Old One by Miska Miles (Little, Brown & Co., 1985)

Annie, Bea, and Chi Chi Delores: A School Day Alphabet by Donna Maurer (Orchard Books, 1998)

Anno's Alphabet by Mitsumasa Anno (HarperCollins Children's Books, 1975)

Anno's Counting Book by Mitsumasa Anno (HarperTrophy, 1986)

Anno's Journey by Mitsumasa Anno (Puffin, 1997)

Arthur's Family Vacation by Marc Brown (Little, Brown and Co., 1995)

Arthur Writes a Story by Marc Brown (Little, Brown Children's Books, 1998)

Aster Aardvark's Alphabet Adventures by Steven Kellogg (Mulberry Books, 1992)

Babar's Family Album by Laurent DeBrunhoff (Random House, Incorporated, 1991)

A Baby Sister for Frances by Russell Hoban (HarperTrophy, 1976)

Bedtime for Frances by Russell Hoban (HarperTrophy, 1976)

Best Friends for Frances by Russell Hoban (HarperTrophy, 1976)

Big Brother Dustin by Alden Carter (Albert Whitman and Company, 1997)

The Biggest Tongue Twister Book in the World by Gyles Brandeth (Sterling, 1983)

A Birthday for Frances by Russell Hoban (HarperTrophy, 1976)

Black and White Rabbit's ABC by Alan Baker (Larousse Kingfisher Chambers, 1999)

Bread and Jam for Frances by Russell Hoban (HarperTrophy, 1993)

Cam Jansen and the Mystery of the Dinosaur Bones by David Adler (Viking Press, 1981)

Charlotte's Web by E. B. White (Harper, 1952)

Chrysanthemum by Kevin Henkes (Morrow, William & Co., 1996)

Clifford the Big Red Dog by Norman Bridwell (Scholastic, Inc., 1985)

Cookie's Week by Cindy Ward (Scholastic Big Books, 1988)

Corduroy by Don Freeman (Puffin, 1976)

Curious George by H. A. Rey (Houghton Mifflin Company, 1973)

Curious George Learns the Alphabet by H. A. Rey (Houghton Mifflin Co., 1973)

Danny and the Dinosaur by Syd Hoff (HarperCollins Children's Books, 1978)

David Goes to School by David Shannon (Scholastic, Inc., 1999)

Doctor DeSoto by William Steig (Sunburst, 1990)

Doctor DeSoto Goes to Africa by William Steig (HarperCollins, 1994)

Dr. Seuss's ABC by Dr. Seuss (Random House Books for Young Readers, 1963)

Dustin's Big School Day by Alden Carter (Albert Whitman, 1999)

Elizabeti's Doll by Stephanie Stuve-Bodeen (Lee and Low Books, 2000)

Encyclopedia Brown Takes the Cake by Donald Sobol (Scholastic, 1991)

Everett Anderson's Christmas Coming by Lucille Clifton (Henry Holt and Co., 1991)

Everett Anderson's Friend by Lucille Clifton (Henry Holt and Co., 1992)

Everett Anderson's Goodbye by Lucille Clifton (Henry Holt and Co., 1983)

Everett Anderson's Nine Months Long by Lucille Clifton (Henry Holt and Co., 1978)

Everett Anderson's Year by Lucille Clifton (Henry Holt and Co., 1992)

Faint Frogs Feeling Feverish and other Terrifically Tantalizing Tongue Twisters by Lilian Obligada (Viking Children's Books, 1986)

Flat Stanley by Jeff Brown (Harper Collins, 1964)

Four Famished Foxes and Fosdyke by Pamela Duncan Edwards (HarperTrophy, 1997)

Franklin Goes to School by Pauline Bourgeois (Scholastic, Inc., 1995)

Franklin in the Dark by Pauline Bourgeois (Scholastic, Inc., 1987)

Franklin's New Friend by Pauline Bourgeois (Scholastic, Inc., 1997)

Franklin Rides a Bike by Pauline Bourgeois (Scholastic, Inc., 1997)

Frederick by Leo Lionni (Dragonfly, 1967)

Goodnight to Annie: An Alphabet Lullaby by Eve Merriam (Hyperion Press, 1999)

Gregory, the Terrible Eater by Mitchell Sharmat (Scholastic, Inc., 1983)

Harold's ABC by Crockett Johnson (HarperCollins Juvenile Books, 1981)

Hattie and the Fox by Mem Fox (Bradbury, 1988; DC Heath Company, 1989; Macmillan, 1987)

Henry and Mudge by Cynthia Rylant (Bradbury, 1991)

Hooper Humperdink by Theodore LeSieg (Random House Books for Young Readers, 1976)

The Hungry Thing by Jan Slepian and Ann Seidler (Scholastic, Inc., 2001)

Ira Sleeps Over by Bernard Waber (Houghton Mifflin Co., 1973)

Johnny Appleseed retold by Steven Kellogg (Scholastic, 1988)

John Henry by Julius Lester (Dial Books, 1994)

Julian's Glorious Summer by Ann Cameron (Random House, 1987)

Leo the Late Bloomer by Robert Kraus (Windmill, 1971)

Lilly's Purple Plastic Purse by Kevin Henkes (Greenwillow, 1996)

The Little Engine That Could by Watty Piper (Grosset & Dunlap, 1976)

The Little Red Hen retold by Janina Domanska (Houghton Mifflin Co., 1991; Macmillan, Inc., 1973)

Madeline by Ludwig Bemelmans (Viking, 1958)

Madeline and the Bad Hat by Ludwig Bemelmans (Viking Press, 1957)

Madeline and the Gypsies by Ludwig Bemelmans (Viking Press, 1959)

Madeline in London by Ludwig Bemelmans (Viking Press, 1961)

Madeline's Rescue by Ludwig Bemelmans (Viking Press, 1953)

Mama Elizabeti by Stephanie Stuve-Bodeen (Lee and Low Books, 2000)

Mirandy and Brother Wind by Patricia McKissack (Knopf, 1988)

Miss Bindergarten Celebrates the 100th Day of Kindergarten by Joseph Slate (Puffin, 2002)

Miss Bindergarten Gets Ready for Kindergarten by Joseph Slate (Puffin, 2001)

Miss Bindergarten Stays Home from Kindergarten by Joseph Slate (Dutton Books, 2000)

Miss Bindergarten Takes a Field Trip with Kindergarten by Joseph Slate (Dutton Books, 2001)

Miss Nelson is Back by Harry Allard (Houghton Mifflin, Co., 1986)

Miss Nelson is Missing by Harry Allard (Scholastic, 1978)

Miss Rumphius by Barbara Cooney (Penguin, 1982)

Miss Spider's ABC by David Kirk (Callaway Editions, 1998)

Moonbear's Books by Frank Asche (Houghton Mifflin School Division, 1993; Simon and Schuster, 1993)

More Stories Julian Tells by Ann Cameron (Yearling, 1989)

Mortimer by Robert Munch (Annick Press Ltd., 1985)

Mufaro's Beautiful Daughters by John Steptoe (HarperTrophy, 1993)

My Brown Bear Barney by Dorothy Butler (HarperCollins Children's Books, 2001)

My Great Aunt Arizona by Gloria Houston (HarperCollins, 1992)

Nettie's Trip South by Ann Turner (Aladdin Paperbacks, 1995)

No, David! by David Shannon (Scholastic, 1998)

Olivia by Ian Falconer (Scholastic, Inc., 2000)

Paddington's ABC by Michael Bond (Puffin, 1996)

Peter's Chair by Ezra Jack Keats (HarperCollins, 1967)

Peter Rabbit's ABC by Beatrix Potter (Viking Press, 1998)

Rachel Parker, Kindergarten Show Off by Ann Martin (Scholastic, Inc., 1993)

Ramona Quimby, Age 8 by Beverly Cleary (HarperTrophy, 1992)

Ramona and Her Father by Beverly Cleary (HarperTrophy, 1999)

Ramona and Her Mother by Beverly Cleary (HarperTrophy, 1990)

Ramona the Brave by Beverly Cleary (HarperTrophy, 1995)

Ramona the Pest by Beverly Cleary (HarperTrophy, 1992)

Rosie's Walk by Pat Hutchins (Simon and Schuster, 1968)

Sarah Morton's Day by Kate Waters (Scholastic, Inc., 1989)

Sarah Plain and Tall by Patricia MacLachlan (HarperCollins, 1985)

Six Sick Sheep: One Hundred Tongue Twisters by Joanna Cole (Beech Tree Books, 1993)

Some of the Days of Everett Anderson by Lucille Clifton (Henry Holt and Co., 1987)

Some Smug Slug by Pamela Duncan Edwards (HarperTrophy, 1998)

Speak English for Us, Marisol! by Karen English (Albert Whitman Co., 2000)

Stanley, Flat Again! by Jeff Brown (HarperTrophy, 2004)

Stellaluna by Janell Cannon (Scholastic, Inc., 1993)

Stevie by John Steptoe (HarperCollins, 1969)

Stories Julian Tells by Ann Cameron (Yearling Books, 1989)

The Story of Ruby Bridges by Robert Coles (Scholastic, Inc., 1995)

Strega Nona by Tomie dePaola (Prentice Hall, 1975)

Sweet Clara and the Freedom Quilt by Deborah Hopkinson (Alfred Knopf, 1993)

Sylvester and the Magic Pebble by William Steig (Simon and Schuster, 1969)

The Tale of Benjamin Bunny by Beatrix Potter (Penguin Books, Ltd., 1993)

The Tale of Peter Rabbit by Beatrix Potter (Scholastic, Inc., 1987)

The Tale of Tom Kitten by Beatrix Potter (Dover, 1995)

There's a Wocket in My Pocket! by Dr. Seuss (Random House Books for Young Readers, 1974)

Things I Like by Anthony Browne (Bantam Doubleday Dell Books for Young Readers, 1997)

A Twister of Twists, A Tangler of Tongues: Tongue Twisters by Alvin Schwartz (Harpercollins Juvenile Books, 1991)

What's Your Name? From Ariel to Zoe by Eve Sanders (Holiday House, 1995)

When Sophie Gets Angry—Really, Really Angry by Molly Bang (Scholastic, Inc., 1999)

Wilfrid Gordon MacDonald Patridge by Mem Fox (Kane/Miller Book Publishers, 1985)

William's Doll by Charlotte Zolotow (Harper, 1972)

Winnie-the-Pooh's ABC by A. A. Milne (Dutton Books, 1995)

Winnie the Pooh's A to Zzzz by Don Ferguson (Disney Press, 1992)

Yeh Shen: A Cinderella Story from China retold by Ai-Ling Louie (Philomel, 1990)

Yolanda's Genius by Carol Fenner (Simon and Schuster, 1995)

Zomo the Rabbit: A Trickster Tale from West Africa by Gerald McDermott (Voyager Books, 1996)

The Names Test of Decoding

Jay Conway	Chuck Hoke
Kimberly Blake	Homer Preston
Cindy Sampson	Ginger Yale
Stanley Shaw	Glen Spencer
Flo Thornton	Grace Brewster
Ron Smitherman	Vance Middleton
Bernard Pendergraph	Floyd Sheldon
Austin Sheperd	Neal Wade
Joan Brooks	Thelma Rinehart
Tim Cornell	Yolanda Clark
Roberta Slade	Gus Quincy
Chester Wright	Patrick Tweed
Wendy Swain	Fred Sherwood
Dee Skidmore	Ned Westmoreland
Troy Whitlock	Zane Anderson
Shane Fletcher	Dean Bateman
Bertha Dale	Jake Murphy
Gene Loomis	

The Names Test

Name _____   Grade _____   Date _____
Teacher _____   Overall Score: _____/70

_____Jay   _____Conway

_____Kimberly   _____Blake

_____Cindy   _____Sampson

_____Stanley   _____Shaw

_____Flo   _____Thornton

_____Ron   _____Smitherman

_____Bernard   _____Pendergraph

_____Austin   _____Sheperd

_____Joan   _____Brooks

_____Tim   _____Cornell

_____Roberta   _____Slade

_____Chester   _____Wright

_____Wendy   _____Swain

_____Dee   _____Skidmore

_____Troy   _____Whitlock

_____Shane   _____Fletcher

_____Bertha

_____Gene

_____Chuck

_____Homer

_____Ginger

_____Glen

_____Grace

_____Vance

_____Floyd

_____Neal

_____Thelma

_____Yolanda

_____Gus

_____Patrick

_____Fred

_____Ned

_____Zane

_____Dean

_____Jake

_____Dale

_____Loomis

_____Hoke

_____Preston

_____Yale

_____Spencer

_____Brewster

_____Middleton

_____Sheldon

_____Wade

_____Rinehart

_____Clark

_____Quincy

_____Tweed

_____Sherwood

_____Westmoreland

_____Anderson

_____Bateman

_____Murphy

	1	2	3	4	5
Aa					
Bb					
Cc					
Dd					
Ee					
Ff					
Gg					
Hh					
Ii					
Jj					
Kk					
Ll					
Mm					
Nn					
Oo					
Pp					
Qq					
Rr					
Ss					
Tt					
Uu					
Vv					
Ww					
Xx					
Yy					
Zz					

Making Names Take-Home Sheet
